BY JAMES HUNEKER

MEZZOTINTS IN MODERN MUSIC (1899)

CHOPIN: THE MAN AND HIS MUSIC (1900)

MELOMANIACS (1902)

OVERTONES (1904)

ICONOCLASTS: A BOOK OF DRAMATISTS (1905)

VISIONARIES (1905)

EGOISTS: A BOOK OF SUPERMEN (1909)

PROMENADES OF AN IMPRESSIONIST (1910)

FRANZ LISZT. ILLUSTRATED (1911)

THE PATHOS OF DISTANCE (1912)

NEW COSMOPOLIS (1915)

IVORY APES AND PEACOCKS (1915)

UNICORNS (1917)

BEDOUINS (1920)

In Preparation

STEEPLEJACK. TWO VOLUMES

CHARLES SCRIBNER'S SONS

MEZZOTINTS IN MODERN MUSIC

MEZZOTINTS
IN MODERN MUSIC

BRAHMS, TSCHAÏKOWSKY, CHOPIN
RICHARD STRAUSS, LISZT
AND WAGNER

BY

JAMES HUNEKER

SIXTH EDITION

NEW YORK
CHARLES SCRIBNER'S SONS
1920

THE SCRIBNER PRESS

Affectionately Inscribed

TO

HENRY EDWARD KREHBIEL

CONTENTS

woes with full throat. Nothing could be wider of the truth. Brahms' music throbs with humanity; with the rich red blood of mankind. He was the greatest contrapuntist after Bach, the greatest architectonist after Beethoven, but in his songs he was as simple, as manly, as tender as Robert Burns. His topmost peaks are tremendously remote, and glitter and gleam in an atmosphere almost too thin for dwellers of the plains; but how intimate, how full of charm, of graciousness are the happy moments in his chamber music!

It is not rashly premature for us to assign to Brahms a place among the immortals. Coming after the last of the most belated romanticists, untouched by the fever for the theatre, a realist with great imagination, both a classicist and a romanticist, he led music back in her proper channels by showing that a phenomenal sense of form and a mastery of polyphony second only to Bach are not incompatible with progress, with the faculty of uttering new things in a new way. Brahms is not a reactionary any more than is Richard Wagner. Neither of these men found what he needed, so one harked back to Gluck and the Greeks, the other to Bach and Beethoven. Consider the massiveness of Brahms' tonal architecture; consider those structures erected after

years of toil; regard the man's enormous fertility of ideas; enormous patience in developing them; consider the ease with which he moves shackled by the most difficult forms — not assumed for the mere sake of the difficult, but because it was the only form in which he could successfully express himself — consider the leavening genius, the active geniality of the man, which militates against pedantry, the dryness of scholasticism and the mere arithmetical music of the kapellmeister; consider the powerful, emotional and intellectual brain of this composer, and then realize that all great works in art are the arduous victories of great minds over great imaginations! Brahms ever consciously schooled his imagination.

Brahms was Brahms' greatest critic. He worked slowly, he produced slowly and, being of the contemplative rather than the active and dramatic type, he incurred the reproach of being phlegmatic, Teutonic, heavy and thick. There is enough sediment in his collected works to give the color of truth to this allegation, but from the richness and the cloudiness of the ferment, is thrown off the finest wine; and how fine, how incomparably noble is a draught of this wine after the thin, acid, frothing and bubbling stuff concocted at every season's musical vintage!

Brahms reminds one of those mediæval architects whose life was a prayer in marble; who slowly and assiduously erected cathedrals, the mighty abutments of which flanked majestically upon mother earth, and whose thin, high pinnacles pierced the blue; whose domes hung suspended between heaven and earth, and in whose nave an army could worship, while in the forest of arches music came and went like the voices of many waters.

He was a living reproach to the haste of a superficial generation. Whatever he wrought he wrought in bronze and for time, not for the hour. He restored to music its feeling for form. He was the greatest symphonist in the constructive sense since Beethoven. He did not fill it with a romantic content as did Schumann, but he never defaced or distorted its flowing contours. Not so great a colorist as Schumann or Berlioz, he was the greatest master of pure line that ever lived. He is accused of not scoring happily. The accusation is true. Brahms does not display the same gracious sense of voicing the needs and capabilities of every orchestral instrument as have Berlioz, Dvorák and Strauss. He is often very muddy, drab and opaque, but his nobility of utterance, his remarkable eloquence and ingenuity in treatment make you forget his

shortcomings in color. But in writing for choral masses, for combinations, such as clarinet and strings, piano, violin and 'cello, or for piano solo, he had few masters. There seems to be a perverse vein in his handling of orchestral color. He gives you the impression of mastery, but writes as if to him the garb, the vestment were naught, and the pure, sweet flesh and form, all.

Brahms had his metaphysical moments when he wrestled with the pure idea as speculatively as a Pascal or a Spinoza. There are minutes in his music when he becomes the purely contemplative mind surveying the nave of the universe; when Giotto's circle is for him an "O Altitudo." It cannot be said, then that Brahms the philosopher, the utterer of cryptic tones, is as interesting as Brahms the composer of the second and third symphonies, the composer of the F minor piano sonata, the F minor piano quintet, the creator of the Schicksalslied, the German Requiem or those exquisite and fragrant flowers, the songs.

Brahms is the first composer since Beethoven to sound the note of the sublime. He has been called austere for this. He has sublimity at times; something that Schumann, Rubinstein, Raff or Tschaïkowsky never quite

compassed. To this is allied that forbidding quality, that want of commonplace sympathy, that lack of personal profile which make his music very often disliked by critic, amateur and professional. He would never make any concessions to popularity; indeed, like Henrik Ibsen, he often goes out of his way to displease! The facile, cheap triumph he despises; he sees all Europe covered with second and third rate men in music, and he notes that they please; their only excuse for living is to give cheap pleasure.

This, and the naturally serious bent of the man, superinduced excessive puritanism. It is a sign of his great culture and flexible mental operations that he grew to study and admire Wagner toward the close of his hard-working life.

Brahms' workmanship is almost impeccable. His mastery of material is as great as Beethoven's and only outstripped by Bach. I have dwelt sufficiently upon his formal and contrapuntal sense. His contribution to the technics of rhythm is enormous. He has literally popularized the cross-relation, rediscovered the arpeggio and elevated it from the lowly position of an accompanying figure to an integer of the melodic phrase. Wagner did the same for the essential turn.

A pure musician, a maker of absolute music, a man of poetic ideals, is Brahms, without thrusting himself forward in the contemporary canvas. Not Berlioz, not Wagner, but the plodding genius Brahms, was elected by destiny to receive upon his shoulders the mantle dropped by Beethoven as he ascended the slope to Parnassus, and the shoulders were broad enough to bear the imposing weight.

They are fast becoming sheeted dead, these great few left us. Who shall fill Wagner's tribune; who shall carve from the harmonic granite imperishable shapes of beauty as did Johannes Brahms?

I

With the death of the master the time has come for an extended and careful investigation of the piano sonatas, the rhapsodies, the intermezzi, the capriccios, the fantasias, the ballades and all the smaller and curious forms left us; a collection, let me preface by declaring, that is more significant and more original than any music since Chopin. Now that I have sounded the challenge I must at once proceed to attenuate it by making some qualifications and one explanation. Brahms

I

THE MUSIC OF THE FUTURE

THE death of Johannes Brahms in 1897 removed from the sparsely settled land of music the last of the immortals; the one whom Bülow justly ranked with Bach and Beethoven; the one upon whom Schumann lavished both praise and prophecy. Not by any wrench of the imagination can we conjure the name of Antonin Dvorák, despite his delightful gift of saying naïve and Slavic things; not by any excess of sentiment can we dower Italy's grand old man Verdi with the title, nor yet France's favorite son, Saint-Saëns; not any one nor all of these three varying talents can be compared to the great, virile man who died in Vienna, the city of his preference but not of his birth.

When the printed list of Brahms' achievements in song, sonata, symphony and choral works of vast proportions is placed before you, amazement at the slow, patient, extraordinary fertility and versatility of the man seizes upon you. It is not alone that he wrote

four symphonies of surpassing merit, two piano concertos, a violin concerto, a double concerto for violin and violoncello, songs, piano pieces, great set compositions like the Song of Destiny and the German Requiem, duos, trios, quartets, quintets, sextets, sestets, all manner of combinations for wood, for wind, for strings and voices; it is the sum total of high excellence, the stern, unyielding adherence to ideals sometimes almost frostily unhuman — in a word, the logical, consistent and philosophic bent of the man's mind — that forces your homage. For half a century he pursued the beautiful in its most elusive and difficult form; pursued it when the fashions of the hour, day and year mocked at such wholesale, undeviating devotion, when form was called old-fashioned, sobriety voted dull, and the footlights had invaded music's realm and menaced it in its very stronghold — the symphony.

When a complete life of Johannes Brahms is written, this trait of fidelity, this marvellous spiritual obstinacy of the man will be lovingly dealt with. There seems to be a notion abroad that because Brahms refused to challenge current tendencies in art and literature he held himself aloof, was remote from humanity, was a bonze of art, a Brahmin, and not a bard chanting its full-blooded wants and

occupies an unsought for and rather unpleasant position in the history of contemporary music. Without his consent he was championed as an adversary of Wagner, and I believe Eduard Hanslick, most brilliant of critics, had something to do with this false attitude. Hanslick hated Wagner and adored Brahms. There you have it; and presently the silly spectacle was observed of two men of straw being pitted one against the other and all musical Europe drawn into a quarrel as absurd as the difference between tweedle-dum and tweedle-dee. Wagner and Brahms are the very antipodes of art, and let it be said most forcibly that art contains easily without violence the various music of two such great artists, although some critics differ from me in this.

Wagner was a great fresco painter, handling his brush with furious energy, magnificence and dramatic intensity. Beside his vast, his tremendous scenery, the music of Brahms is all brown, all gray, all darkness, and often small. It is not imposing in the operatic sense, and it reaches results in a vast, slow, even cold blooded manner, compared with the reckless haste of Richard of the Footlights. One is all showy externalization, a seeker after immediate and sensuous effects;

the other, one of those reserved, self-contained men who feels deeply and watches and waits. In a word, Wagner is a composer for the theatre, with all that the theatre implies, and sought to divert — and nearly succeeded — the tide of music into theatrical channels.

Brahms is for the concert room, a symphonist, a song writer and, above all, a German. I wish to emphasize this point of nationality. Wagner was the Celt, with a dash of the Oriental in his blood, and he bubbled and foamed over with primal power, but it was not the reticent, grave power of the Teuton, who, as Amiel puts it, gathers fuel for the pile and allows the French to kindle it. Whether it was Wagner's early residence in Paris, or perhaps some determining pre-natal influence, he surely had a vivacity, an esprit, imagination and a grace denied to most of his countrymen, Heine excepted. You may look for these qualities in Brahms, but they are rarely encountered. Sobriety, earnestness, an intensity that is like the blow of a steam hammer, and a rich, informing spirit are present, and undoubted temperament also, but as there are temperaments and temperaments, so the temperament of Brahms differs from the temperament of Wagner, the temperament of Chopin and the temperament of

Liszt. There is a remoteness, a sense of distance in his music that only long pursued study partially dissipates. He is a chilly friend at first, but the clasp of the hand is true, if it is not always charmful. I find the same difficulty in Beethoven, in Ibsen, in Gustave Flaubert, and sometimes in Browning, but never in Schumann and never in Schubert. As Emerson said of Walt Whitman, there must have been a "long foreground somewhere" to the man, and that foreground is never wholly traversed with Brahms.

You will ask me what is there then so fascinating in this austere, self-centred man, whose music at first hearing suggests both a latter-day Bach and a latter-day Beethoven?

The answer is simply this: Brahms is a profound thinker; his chilliness is in manner, not matter; he is a thinker, but he also feels sincerely, deeply, and maybe, as Ehlert says, feels with his head and thinks with his heart. He is hardly likely to become popular in this generation, yet he is a very great artist and a great composer. Von Bülow was enjoying a little of his perverse humor when he spoke of the three Bs. Brahms is not knee-high to Bach or Beethoven, yet he is their direct descendant, is of their classic lineage, although a belated romanticist, and the only man we

see fit to mention after the two kings of the tone art.

This does not mean that Schumann, Berlioz, Tschaïkowsky, Liszt, Wagner and the rest are not as great, or even greater, but simply that certain immutable and ineluctable laws of art are understood by Brahms, who prefers to widen in his own fashion the beaten path rather than conquer new ones.

In 1853 Schumann wrote his New Paths, and Brahms became known. Schumann had doubtless certain affinities with the young man of twenty, and he also recognized his strangeness, for in the first bar of Brahms you are conscious of something new, something strange. It is not in the form, not in the idea, not in the modulation, rhythmical change, curve of harmonic line, curve of melodic line, yet it is in all these that there lurks something new, something individual. This same individuality caused Schumann to rub his eyes when he heard the C major sonata, and made Liszt grow enthusiastic when he read the scherzo in E flat minor.

I quite agree with Spitta that it is a mistake to suppose that Brahms worked altogether on the lines of Bach, Beethoven, Mozart and Schumann. I called him a belated romanticist a moment ago because much of the

content of his music is romantic, and in his latter days excessively modern. It is because of his adherence to classic forms, and his harking back to the methods of the sixteenth century, that the music of Brahms so often misleads both critic and public. Spitta dilates most admirably upon the richness and variety of his tonality, by his reversion to almost forgotten manners and modes; the Doric, his characteristic use of the octave, the sharpening of minor thirds and sixths, his remarkable employment of the chord of the sixth, sharp transitions in modulation, the revival of playing common time against triple time, and the use of rhythms and tonalities that are vague, indeterminate and almost misleading, without damage to the structural values and beauty of the music.

Then in form Brahms knows the canon as no other composer. Listen to Spitta: "Schumann had already seriously studied and revised the canon, which had sunk to the level of an amusing exercise; Brahms interested himself in its stricter construction and used it in a greater variety of forms. The extension and diminution of the melody again — that is to say, the lengthening of the strain by doubling the value of the notes, or shortening it by diminishing their value,

which was such an important element of form in the fifteenth and sixteenth centuries, came to light again for the first time with all its innate musical vitality when Brahms took it up, and even in his earliest works (for instance, op. 3, no. 2) showed how thoroughly he understood it. The same is to be said of the method of inversion, the derivation of a new melody from the former by reversing the intervals. When the use of such 'artifices'—as they were called with an amazing misapprehension of the very essence of music—had from time to time been admitted, they had always been restricted to what was termed a 'Gelehrten Satz'; that is to say, they were worked out as school exercises and formed no part of the artist's living work. But with Brahms they pervade all his music, and find a place as much in the piano sonata and the simple ballad as in the grand choral pieces with orchestral accompaniments.

"The basso ostinato, with the styles pertaining to it—the Passacaglia and the Ciacona—resume their significance for the first time since Bach's time, and their intrinsic importance is enhanced by the support of the symphonic orchestra."

And with all this, as Ehlert truly says, "Brahms' art undoubtedly rests upon the

golden background of Bach's purity and concentration."

I know it may be questioned whether Brahms belongs to the romantic camp, but while he has absorbed with giant-like ease the individualization of voices and the severity of Bach, yet he is a modern among moderns. How modern, you will discover if you play first the early music of Schumann, or the music of Chopin's middle period, and then take up the B minor rhapsody or some of the later fantasias. Brahms then seems so near, so intimate, so full of vitality, while the romantic music has a flavor of the rococo, of the perfume of the salon, of that stale and morbid and extravagant time when the classics were defied and Berlioz thought to be a bigger man than Beethoven. But all passes, and time has left us of Schumann's piano music, the Symphonic Variations, the F sharp minor and the F minor sonatas, the fantasy in C and the concerto, while the mists are slowly enveloping most of Chopin's earlier music. Doubtless the studies, preludes, the F minor fantasy, one polonaise, the barcarolle, the F minor ballade, the C sharp minor and the B minor scherzi will live forever, and I am not so sure that I could predict the same of the piano music of Brahms.

However, escape this fact we cannot: Brahms is our most modern music maker, and if, as Edward MacDowell says, Tschaïkowsky's music always sounds better than it is, the music of Brahms is often better than it sounds!

Now I have made all of my qualifications, and my single explanation is this: I am not a reckless Brahms worshipper. There is much in his music that repels, and I have often studied his piano with knitted brow. After the exquisite, poetic tenderness of Chopin, the overflowing romance of Schumann, the adorable melody of Schubert, and the proud pose of Weber — who prances by you on gayly and gorgeously caparisoned arpeggios — Brahms may sound cold, formal, and much of the mathematician, but strip him of his harsh rind, taste the sweetness, the richness, the manliness of the fruit and you will grow enthusiastic.

It would be easy and it would look imposing for me to map out three styles in Brahms, as De Lenz did with the piano sonatas of Beethoven. But it would be manifestly absurd, for as much as Brahms gained in mastery and variety in his later years, yet he was more Brahms in his op. 1 than was Chopin in *his* op. 2 — the famous La Ci Darem, the variations that led Schumann to his famous discovery. Take, for instance, the E flat minor scherzo, so different from Chopin's glorious one in the same key in the B flat minor sonata. This scherzo of Brahms is an op. 4, and he played it for Schumann during the historical visit to Düsseldorf. It has in it something of Chopin, more in color than idea, and it is so free, so flowing, so plastic, so happily worked out, that it must have come upon Liszt and Schumann as something absolutely new. Yet I find it old-fashioned compared to his op. 116 or 117 or 118 or 119. Even the rhapsodies strike a new note, so I may without impropriety, and I hope without pedantry, make a general division of his piano music into two groups. In the first I include the three sonatas, the scherzo — which is a separate opus — the variations, the four ballades, and the Walzer, op. 39. There is then a skip to op. 76 before we encounter solo music, and here I begin my second group with the eight capriccios and intermezzi. Then follow the two rhapsodies, and until op. 116 we encounter no piano soli. With op. 119 Brahms' contributions to piano literature end. The two books of technical studies, fifty-one in all, will be considered, as will the Hungarian dances, arranged by the composer from the orchestral partition.

This grouping is purely arbitrary, and I warn you that the composer cannot be pinned down to any such cataloguing, for we find in his second sonata, the one in F sharp minor, stuff that is kin to his latest works and in some of his new fantasies a reversion to the Brahms of the Ballades.

Regarding his technics I can only recommend to you a close study of the music. There is much that is unusual side by side with the most trite patterns. He has a special technic, sudden extensions, he is fond of tenths and twelfths — the interlocking — for instance, in the capriccio in D minor with its devilish rhythms and cross accent, and the spreading of the triplet over two bars of three-four time — the rapid flights in chord playing — all these things require a firm seat in the saddle, hands with ten well individualized voices and a light wrist. The best preparation for Brahms is Bach, then the toccata of Schumann, and then the Brahms studies. There are scales in Brahms' music, but not many. His passage work is of the most solid character, broken chords, double notes, especially thirds and sixths, and few arpeggios. The triolen he has idealized as

did Wagner the essential turn, and his accompaniment figures are always simple, indeed vital parts of the composition. Brahms is not a great original melodist. Like Schumann his melodies can hardly be divorced from his harmonies. He had his moments of ecstatic lyrism, and I can show you many specimens of perfect melodies in his piano music. He is not always gloomy, forbidding, cross-grained and morbid. Take the first movement of the D major symphony, the slow movement of the F minor sonata, some of the songs, the horn trio, and tell me if this man cannot unbend the bow, say lovely, gracious things and be even nimble of wit and of gait?

Regarding Brahms' muddy orchestration, this is a question I leave to my betters. Scored in the high, violent purples and screaming scarlets of Richard Strauss, the grave, reflective, philosophic accents of the C minor and E minor symphonies would be as foolishly attired as Socrates the day Plato insisted upon his donning the fashionable costume of Athens' gayest youth.

Touching the muddiness and heaviness of the doubled basses of the piano music, I may say that it is a matter of taste. Some pianists, indeed some musicians, do not care for a

broad foundational bass. The arpeggio figure in the left hand has been worked to death, and it is a relief to find Brahms making his accompaniment figures an integer of the piece itself.

He has dealt the death blow to the tyranny of virtuoso passage work. No composer dare follow him and expect to build up, to advance, who employs passage work for the sake of mere display of the desire to dazzle. Every note of Brahms belongs to the framework, to the musical scheme. He is more Hellenic than Mozart in his supreme economy, and not even Beethoven is more devoted to formal beauty. He has not much sense of humor, and the scherzi, while not being as ironical or as brilliant as Chopin's, are none the less misnomers. In his working-out sections the marvellously inventive and logical brain of Brahms is seen at its culminating splendor. As free in his durchführungsatz as the wind, he has emancipated the sonata form in the matter of tonality and in the matter of emotional content. Excepting Chopin and Wagner, no composer has ever exhibited such versatility in the choice of keys. His use of mixed scales — a result of his studies in Hungarian music — gives his music its intensely foreign coloring. There you have

Brahms, a German, a follower of Bach and Beethoven as regards polyphony and form, a reticent romanticist and a lover of certain colorings that I call foreign, because they are certainly not European. He has appropriated the Magyar spirit with infinitely more success than Liszt — take the last movement of the B flat major concerto — and when I say Magyar I mean almost Asiatic.

Brahms has in the piano concerto freed the form forever, while writing within the limits of that form. His two concertos are concertos, not rhapsodies and fantasies, and the solo instrument, instead of being a brilliant but loquacious gabbler of glittering platitudinous passage work, is now the expounder of the musical idea and the stanch ally of the orchestra.

Despite his vast knowledge, an almost magical erudition, there is a certain looseness and want of finish about Brahms that is refreshing in these days of Art for Art's sake and the apotheosis of the cameo cutter. He is never a little master, although he can work exceeding fine and juggle for you by the hour the most gorgeous balls of bitter-sweet virtuosity. He is not, I say, always the pedant, and he can be as dull as ditch water two times out of ten. He has his feminine side — his songs —

but in the main he is a muscular male, not given to over-expansion and not always companionable.

I agree with Mr. Edgar Kelley that his music is not always klaviermässig, but the same objection was urged against Beethoven, Schumann and even Chopin! I prefer a granitic bass, although the doubling is not always agreeable. But Schumann and Chopin were sinners in this respect, especially the former. That is why I recommend the great toccata in C as a preliminary study to Brahms. To sincere antagonists of Brahms, such as Mr. Henry T. Finck, I can only say that not every poet is to one's taste. Browning's Sordello is crabbed music after Tennyson, and Swinburne cloying, after Matthew Arnold or Arthur Hugh Clough. But the inner, the spiritual ear is longer enamored of the harmonies of a Brahms or Bach than of the sonorous splendors of Wagner or Verdi. It is the still, small voice discerned in a Brahms adagio or a Chopin prelude that abides by us and consoles when the music of the theatre seems superficial and garish. Those who do not care for Brahms — let them choose their own musical diet. There are, however, some of us who prefer his lean to other composers' fat. The light that beats about his throne is

a trifle dry at times, but it is at least white, and the time comes to all when the chromatic ceases to make thrall, and line, not color, seems the more beautiful. Therefore do not follow me further if you are a genuine anti-Brahmsianer. You might hear unpalatable truths.

II

Brahms must have been completely worn out when he presented his credentials to Schumann one memorable October morning in 1853. He had walked part of the way to Düsseldorf because his money was gone, and not being of Heinrich Heine's mercurial temperament, he probably did not think of the witty poet's " fine plums between Jena and Weimar," but to Schumann's questioning, answered by playing the C major sonata, his op. 1.

Little wonder Schumann, great artist and great critic, should have declared of it that it was " music the like of which he had never heard before," and proclaimed the shy, awkward youth a master. It was enough to turn the head of anyone but a Brahms, who had just played at Weimar. Through Liszt's golden generosity the young man played in concert his op. 4, the scherzo in E flat minor, which Liszt praised warmly, and its romantic flush and passion caused Brahms' name to be added as a strong, promising one to the revolutionary and romantic party.

We heard Von Bülow interpret the sonata in C when he played here last. It is a sterling work, clearly, forcibly presented, the keynote of the opening movement being virile determination. Here was a young giant who delighted in wrestling with his material, who enjoyed its very manipulation. You can see the big muscles in his broad back bulge out to the bursting point, for the task he had set himself was no facile one. Nurtured on Bach and Beethoven, the new music-maker started out full of the ideals of these two masters, and you are not surprised by the strong and strange resemblance to Beethoven's op. 106, the Hammer-Klavier sonata in B flat. This resemblance is more than rhythmic, but it stops after the enunciation of the first subject, for following a subsidiary the lyric theme is surely Brahms', while the working-out section, which begins with the use of the second theme, is simply extraordinary for a beginner. It reveals all the devices of counterpoint used in the freest fashion, and doubtless led Schumann to class the composer as a romanticist, for learning never moved about with such airy fantasy. Doubtless, too, Schumann's monophonic sins rose before him in the presence of this genial polyphony. Just compare the Abegg variations with the slow movement of this sonata and you may realize the superior educational advantages enjoyed by Brahms.

The andante is built on the theme of an old German Minnelied, the words of which begin so: "Verstohlen geht der Mond, blau, blau, Blümelein." The left hand sounds eight single tones: then both hands, imitating the chorus, play in transparent four-part harmony. The effect is simplicity itself and seems to upspring from the very soil of the Fatherland; Brahms takes his subject and treats it with sweet reticence, even to the coda, one of his most charming. The scherzo leaps boldly into the middle of things, a habit of Brahms, and is Beethovian in its economy of material and sharply defined outlines. The trio is very melodious; the whole movement impresses you as the work of a musical thinker. The finale in strict form interests me less, although there is a characteristic song theme. The entire sonata overflows with vigor and imagination.

The second sonata, op. 2, in F sharp minor, brings us from the study chamber to more stirring life. The design of the first movement is large. We get the first touch of the grand manner — and Brahms is genuinely dramatic, the drama of the physical plane as well as of the psychical. There can be no mistaking the accents of the introduction, with its well sustained element of suspense, its skips — a familiar feature in the Brahms piano music — and the thundering octaves. Here is virtuosity in plenty for you in the first two pages, and if after playing pages three and four you find Brahms deficient in romantic warmth, then let us unclasp hands and seek you some well-footed byway.

This second theme is nobility itself, and written in full chords; the harmonies are not so dispersed as you might imagine; the effect is sonorous and beautiful; of darkness there is none, and the clarity of the design is admirable. The polyphonic branches of this great trunk are finely etched against a dramatic background, and this most energetic of allegros has no savor of Schumann's sonata in the same key; and yet the temptation to imitate must have been well-nigh irresistible to a neophyte. The very key color might tempt even the most strong headed, but Brahms was too prepossessed with his own thoughts, and so we get a movement that is a great step in advance over the first sonata.

Both the second and third movements are built on the same thematic idea, an extremely simple one of four notes, B, C, D, A sharp, with an answer. The key is B minor. The scherzo is extremely ingenious. The trio is in D, and abounds in harmonic and rhythmic variety. The last movement actually contains in the introduction a scale run. The movement itself reminds me, but in an odd, perverted way, of the second movement of Beethoven's sonata, op. 90, in E minor. The finale contains a big climax, also in scales that look very un-Brahmsian. This sonata in F sharp minor is much more significant than its predecessor.

When you have reached the third sonata in F minor, op. 5, the broad, far-reaching uplands of the composer's genius are clearly discerned, for his two earlier efforts in the sonata form, despite their mastery of technics of form, still remain grounded on the territory of Beethoven and even of Schumann. But in the third sonata we are impressed by a certain passionate grandeur and originality of utterance, a freedom and elasticity of movement, a more nervous fibre, a deeper feeling, a deeper fire. I consider — and remember that my single opinion is nothing as compared to the number of them that believe the same — that in the F minor sonata the most beautiful in the genius of Brahms has flowered. The first allegro is heaven-storming, the second theme, oh! so like the master at his best, while page after page unrolls for us the warp and woof of the most logical musical imagination since Bach. Brahms not a melodist! Read that first movement, and if that does not convince you, play the andante in A flat, the most exquisite lyrical thing he has ever penned for piano. Its motto is from Sternau, "Der Abend dämmert, das Mondlicht scheint," and the picture is magical in its tender beauty and suggestiveness. It harks back to the old world romance, to some moonlit dell, wherein love hovers for a night, and about all is the mystery of sky and wood.

Take the poco piu lento, in four-sixteenth time, with its recurring sixths, divided so amorously for two hands; with any one else but Brahms this well used interval would be banal, but he knows its possibilities and the entire section with the timid-sweet chords of the tenth evokes a mood seldom met with. Moonlight may be hinted at, as in the middle part, the trio of Chopin's scherzo in B minor. Here is an analogous picture. The coda has always brought back to me Hans Sachs' "Dem Vogel der heut' sang." Yes, Brahms knew his Wagner, too, and no doubt would have laughed in his gnomic beard if you had mentioned the mood-resemblance. Moriz Moszkowski has also seized the same idea, for in his Momen Musicale in C sharp minor he has for a second subject this identical one. It comes originally from Schumann's song, Sonntags am Rhein. The resemblance to the Meistersinger lies principally in the third bar of this coda in the upward inflection. Brahms has treated the entire movement with unsurpassable poetry. In the scherzo which follows he is at his best; a certain grim, diabolic humor being hurled at you as if some being, ambuscaded in Parnassus, took pleasure in showering heavy masses of metal on your unprotected head. The tempo suggests the valse, but an epical valse. This is the greatest scherzo ever composed by Brahms, and the trio takes us back to Beethoven.

In the intermezzo — the Rückblick — the resemblance to Mendelssohn has not escaped Mr. Fuller-Maitland. It is in the key of B flat minor, and is a far-off echo, as if heard through sad, falling waters, of the theme of the andante. The bass is naught else — and this no writer has dared or perhaps thought necessary to notice — than the Funeral March from Mendelssohn's Songs Without Words. The familiar triplet in thirty-second notes emphasizes the similarity, but what a vast distance there is in this tragic page, full of veiled suffering, and the pretty and elegiac march of Mendelssohn!

The finale is strong and full of characteristic agitation. The technics throughout are Beethoven's, but a latter day Beethoven. Heavy chord work, no scales, passages, extreme clearness and plenty of involved rhythms. The character of this sonata is lofty, not altogether serene, but the strong, self-contained soul is there; it is music for men of strong nerves and big hearts, and not for the sick or shallow brained.

There is a piano sonata arranged from the sextet in B flat for strings. It is not the arrangement of Brahms, but by Robert Keller, and is not difficult. It is chiefly interesting because of its being an agreeable and available score of the famous chamber music.

The scherzo in E flat minor is a separate opus — four in the published list. Whether it was ever intended to fit in the more extended scheme we do not know; probably Dr. Hanslick could enlighten us. It is the airiest and loveliest thing imaginable, and

while the composer solves some very pretty canonic problems, the learning is never burdensome. As if Brahms had resolved to let gravity go hence, he wings his way in graceful plastic flight, not forgetting in his second theme to give Grieg the melodic idea for the first allegro of the popular piano concerto. There are two trios, both interesting, the second more to my taste, because of its lyricism. Just here we get a Chopin touch in the C sharp minor theme, with its rolling, arpeggiated basses. The development and return of the subject is most happily managed. Why this piano piece does not figure often upon the programmes of recitals is only to be explained by the hide-bound, timid conservatism of the average concert pianist. I swear to you I firmly believe that the decadence of the piano recital — and who can deny that it is not in decay — is to be ascribed to the fact that the scheme of the programmes is so lugubriously monotonous. Bach-Liszt, Beethoven sonata, Chopin or Schumann group, Liszt Hungarian rhapsody, there you have it season after season; whereas, a far-seeing pianist might introduce an occasional novelty by Brahms, or indeed by any one, and with the thin edge of the wedge once in, a complete topsy-turveying of old methods would ensue,

and what a boon would it not be for the concert-goer!

The ballades do not next claim our notice by right of opus, for the variations, op. 9, follow the sonata in F minor, ops. 6, 7 and 8 being given over to two sets of six songs and the familiar piano trio in B. But I prefer treating the six books of variations together. The ballades, four in number, are labelled op. 10. The first in D minor has the narrative quality imperatively demanded by the form, but Brahms has his own notions about the time beat, and so we find the first two in common time instead of the usual triple measure. Thus there is a gain in dignity and stateliness. The D minor ballade is rather a lugubrious work divided into an andante and allegro. The empty fifth harmony in the bass, the slow progression in the treble, gives the theme a mournful and Gaelic character. In runic tones the tale of Herder's Scottish ballade, Edward, is told, and the dead hero home to his love is brought. The section in D, with its triplets, gives us some surcease from the gloom, although there is a peculiarly hollow effect in the triplet imitation in the bass. This ballade is almost sinister in coloring and touches of Brahms' irony are present. It is

extended form and more florid content of the Chopin ballades, which are in the main unapproachable. With Brahms there is no suspicion of a set piece; in Chopin the virtuoso often faces us. It is, after all, the German and the Pole, and further commentary would be superfluous.

And now to the piano variations. Brahms is not only the greatest variationist of his times, but with Bach and Beethoven the greatest of all times. Oddly enough, we must join Brahms' name with the two earlier masters whenever we approach the serious, the severe side of the art. I refer to Spitta's pertinent remark about the variation form.

The old variation form, above all, he says, is brought out from the treasures of the old composers, and glorified in his hands. Brahms' variations are something quite different from what had been commonly known by that name. Their prototype is Bach's aria with thirty variations, and this work is an elaboration of the form known as the passacaglia. In this the determining idea is not the addition of figures or of various accompaniments to the theme or melody, but the persistent identity of the bass. This continues the same through all the variations;

restatement of the idea; in the second the bass becomes very important; the third calls for no special mention, but the fourth and fifth are bold, capricious, and the sixth very brilliant; the seventh is very short, but pregnant, and the eighth is superb. A pedal bass supports the faintly whispered theme, which is heard in waving rhythms, as the sobbing of the wind through the trees. In Paderewski's strongly individualized Variations in A minor there is a variation built in this fashion, and you may find, in Tschaïkowsky's interesting Variations in F, another example.

In the famous ninth variation of this set we find Brahms indulging in a very delicate and ingenious fancy. He has combined with the original theme the entire arpeggio work of Schumann's little piece in B minor from the Bunten Blättern, op. 99, no. 5. As Spitta says, how thoroughly Brahms had thought out the spirit of the variation is seen in the fact that he is fond of interchanging the modulatory relations of the two phrases of the theme. The place where this generally occurs is at the beginning of the second part; but also in the second half of the first part. The digressions, more or less important, which he admits, are always so chosen that the effect of the newly introduced key approximately answers to that

extended form and more florid content of the Chopin ballades, which are in the main unapproachable. With Brahms there is no suspicion of a set piece; in Chopin the virtuoso often faces us. It is, after all, the German and the Pole, and further commentary would be superfluous.

And now to the piano variations. Brahms is not only the greatest variationist of his times, but with Bach and Beethoven the greatest of all times. Oddly enough, we must join Brahms' name with the two earlier masters whenever we approach the serious, the severe side of the art. I refer to Spitta's pertinent remark about the variation form.

The old variation form, above all, he says, is brought out from the treasures of the old composers, and glorified in his hands. Brahms' variations are something quite different from what had been commonly known by that name. Their prototype is Bach's aria with thirty variations, and this work is an elaboration of the form known as the passacaglia. In this the determining idea is not the addition of figures or of various accompaniments to the theme or melody, but the persistent identity of the bass. This continues the same through all the variations;

upon that, a free treatment is worked out— not, however, excluding an occasional reference to the original melody. Beethoven so far adhered to the usually accepted form as to restrict the supremacy of the bass to alternate use with variations in the melody, and Schumann followed his example. This form was not adopted by other great masters, and even Beethoven and Schumann only occasionally used it. Brahms, so rich in inventive combinations, stands nearer to Bach than to Beethoven, but has much of Beethoven's freer style of treatment. Augmentation or diminution of the phrases forming the theme are a manner of variation never used by Beethoven, and employed by Brahms only in the variations in the two first sonatas, and in the independent Air with Variations, op. 9. In this it is often surprisingly ingenious, but he must have thought the process incompatible with his strict sense of form, just as he gave up changes of key from one variation to the next, which Schumann often used and Beethoven allowed himself only once (op. 34).

The first set of variations made by Brahms is on a theme of Schumann in F sharp minor. It is a beautiful theme, marked Ziemlich Langsam, and is familiar to all Schumann stu-

dents; for it is, if I remember aright, the first of the Albumblätter. These variations dimly reveal the inexhaustible fancy of the composer. He views his subject from every possible viewpoint; he sees it as a philosopher, he grimly contemplates it as a cynic; he sings it in mellifluous accents, he plays with it, teases it contrapuntally, and alternately freezes it into glittering stalactites and disperses it in warm, violet-colored vapors. The theme is never lost; it lurks behind formidable ambushes of skips, double notes and octaves, or it slaps you in the face, its voice threatening, its size ten times increased by its harmonic garb. It wooes, caresses, sighs, smiles, coquets, and sneers—in a word, a modern magician weaves for you the most delightful stories imaginable, all the while damnably distracting your attention and harrowing your nerves by spinning in the air polyphonic cups, saucers, plates and balls, and never letting them for a moment reach the earth.

Louis Ehlert believes that the Brahms variation was begotten by a classical father, the thirty-two variations of Beethoven; and a romantic mother, the Symphonic Studies of Schumann. The comparison is apt enough. The first variation on the F sharp minor theme of Schumann seems more like a quiet

restatement of the idea; in the second the bass becomes very important; the third calls for no special mention, but the fourth and fifth are bold, capricious, and the sixth very brilliant; the seventh is very short, but pregnant, and the eighth is superb. A pedal bass supports the faintly whispered theme, which is heard in waving rhythms, as the sobbing of the wind through the trees. In Paderewski's strongly individualized Variations in A minor there is a variation built in this fashion, and you may find, in Tschaïkowsky's interesting Variations in F, another example.

In the famous ninth variation of this set we find Brahms indulging in a very delicate and ingenious fancy. He has combined with the original theme the entire arpeggio work of Schumann's little piece in B minor from the Bunten Blättern, op. 99, no. 5. As Spitta says, how thoroughly Brahms had thought out the spirit of the variation is seen in the fact that he is fond of interchanging the modulatory relations of the two phrases of the theme. The place where this generally occurs is at the beginning of the second part; but also in the second half of the first part. The digressions, more or less important, which he admits, are always so chosen that the effect of the newly introduced key approximately answers to that

produced by the original key of the preceding or following phrase. Even the cadenzas appear altered from this point of view.

In the tenth the bass is used in the upper part, and the subject derived from the diminishing to half or quarter notes of the beginning of the subject; the essential harmonies are preserved in the same succession, while the subject is worked out to fill the required measures, so the reflections of the theme are diverse and glancing.

The eleventh variation is brief, but full of meat, and in it the main idea almost disappears in cloudy octaves, in which an occasional middle voice may be faintly discerned. The twelfth is a heart-breaker, and bold to extremes. The coda ends in a whirlwind of skips, and the wonder-working of the Paganini studies is dimly presaged.

No. 13 is in the shape of a toccata in double notes, and is capital; but my favorite variation, over which you may dream soft, summer night dreams, is the next, the fourteenth. This is a true nocturne, and its hesitating tones, over an undulating bass, tell of the dear, dead Chopin, lying near Bellini, in Père la Chaise.

Variation fifteen is in G flat and in the Lydian mode, the coda-finale is as if Brahms feared to part from his theme and took a lingering leave taking. These variations are worthy of the deepest study.

III

The Walzer, op. 39, were not written first for two hands, but for four. The composer arranged them afterward for solo purposes. They are divine specimens of the dance, and I prefer them even to Rubinstein, and that is saying much, for the Russian has left many admirable examples.

Any comparison with the Chopin valse is of course out of the question. Chopin wrote, as Liszt truthfully said, for countesses, and in his aristocratic measures we feel the swirl of silken skirts, divine the perfume of the fashionable salon and hear the soft pulsations of delicate, half uttered confidences. The room rustles with the patter of beauty's feet, but after all it is a drawing room; not a breath of the open is there.

There are some of the Chopin valses that are not only mediocre, but positively bad. Take the first, the one in E flat, is it not actually vulgar? And the one in A flat that follows is not much better. The A minor valse is elegiac, even unto the Mendelssohnian point. It is when the A flat valse, op. 42, is reached that we get a taste of the true Chopin. This with the one in C sharp minor, the posthumous valse in E minor and the delightfully developed dance in A flat are Chopin at his dancing best. The D flat valse is something to be avoided, simply because of the woful way it has been misrepresented by pianists. I don't allude to double-noting the unfortunate piece, but to the erroneous fashion of playing the first section too fast and the second too slow. Georges Mathias, of Paris, a genuine Chopin pupil, said that the master took the tempo rather moderately, making an accelerando on the up run, ending with a little click on B flat. The rubato, so M. Mathias declared, was indescribably beautiful; therefore, unless the Chopin tradition is carried out, let the Valse de Chien rest its tiresome little bark in peace. With the E flat nocturne, it has become a nuisance.

The musical content of the Chopin valse is a certain suavity, distinctive grace, charming rhythm and aristocratic melody, and it is safe to say that few of these qualities can be found in the Brahms Walzer. But as is the case with Schubert, Brahms dances more poetically, and always in the open air. Sometimes the round verge of the sun blazes overhead in the blue, and you hear the muscular jolt of large limbed men and women taking their pleasure heartily, then the aromatic night of the forest encompasses you, and the sound of dancing is heard, but afar. Poetry is in the air and passion too, and exquisite is the sound and exquisite the suggestion.

Take the first dance of the op. 39. It is in the key of B, and harmonized in the lustiest, freest fashion imaginable. It opens boldly, joyously, with the decisiveness we know so well in the preambule to Schumann's Carneval. It is but a page long, and a small page at that, but there is no mistaking its worth.

The second valse in E has an entrancing lilt, marked dolce; it is well named. The mood is nocturnal, the color subdued, but none the less full of glancing richness. Then follow two tiny gems, as precious almost as some of Chopin's preludes. The one is in the warm and neglected key of G sharp minor, the other in E minor. The first has the pulse beat of Chopin, the second is Hungarian and lovely, and the brace of harmonic progressions at the close is worth living for.

If there could be such a thing as a sacred valse, then No. 5 of the series is sacred. In the key of E, you can sense the valse, but the theme is serious to gravity, just as a Chopin scherzo is a tragic poem. One feels like echoing Robert Schumann's "How is gravity to clothe itself if jest goes about in dark veils?"

C sharp major is the key of No. 6, and has a touch of the fantastic element that we find in the variations. No. 7 in C sharp minor-major is full of harmonic variety. My two favorites of the set are the valses in B flat and D minor. Both are poems. The one in B flat is a proof positive of Brahms' "geniality." In a small piano piece by the Russian Liadow, the same melodic and rhythmic idea is utilized; even the pretty modulation from B flat to D flat is not overlooked. Then on the page opposite in the valse in D minor, Brahms pilfers boldly from Schumann. In the Pièces Caractéristiques (Die Davidsbündler) No. 18, in C, certainly prompted Brahms, but with what ease and variety has he not handled the other man's theme! It is like a sigh, an unshed tear, and is more Brahms than it is Schumann.

By a clever suspension we are at once led to dance No. 10 in G. The next valse in B minor might have been written by Schubert. It is a charming pendant to the Momen

Musicale, or is it an impromptu in F minor?

There are sixteen in all and I have briefly indicated the principal ones, although there is yet another in the key of G sharp minor and a delightful one in A flat, No. 15. This has the true tang of Brahms, the amiability, the large, sweet nature, the touch of life that we call universal when we find it in Shakespeare. Brahms is far from being a poet of the universal, for he is too German, lacks marked profile and is more the philosopher than the bard. Yet has he something of fulness of life; the strenuous ideality that is always found in world-poets.

Remember, too, that I am considering the man from the points of view of his piano works. Consider the great German Requiem, the C minor symphony, the D minor piano concerto, before you class this composer as a specialist working within well defined limitations. I dislike playing the part of an advocate when all should be so clear in the Brahms question, but I do so because of his supreme indifference to what anyone thought of his theory and practice, and also because of the cloud thrown over him by his warmest enemies and most misguided admirers. That he lives, that he gains continually in strength, and this, too, in spite of the Brahmsianer, is a satisfactory guarantee of his genius.

Let me quote for you what Louis Ehlert — by no means a Brahmsianer — wrote of the Walzer: "Having in time assumed an ordinary and most material character, dance music has been led back to the domain of high art by Schubert and Chopin. Dancing may be accomplished in many ways: passionately, indifferently, distractedly or symbolically. The symbolic dancer will introduce in his motions the poetic idea underlying the dance; that is, the fleeting, half confidential, and yet not binding, contact of one person with another of the opposite sex, a sort of rhythmic dialogue without words. And Brahms possessed the gift of substantiating his mastery in this field by the charm of half revealed sentiment, by the modest denial of the scarcely uttered confession and by his power of rendering the wildest yearnings speechless with confusion.

"At times, it is true, he handles his subject in a more decided manner, but the most beautiful among his waltzes are those whose cheeks are tinged with blushes. Brahms carried the freshness of youth into his later years, and blushes are peculiarly becoming to him. His sweetest melodies are merely tinted with a rosy hue; they do not possess the deep, summery complexion of Schubert's. The small opus has become the ancestor of a small literature, and many of our contemporary musicians have walked in the way of the Brahms waltzes."

Elsewhere he says of the Love Song Waltzes for mixed quartet, with four-handed piano accompaniment: "Schumann and Chopin have themselves scarcely succeeded in arriving at a more intellectual and poetic form of the dance." And remember Ehlert wrote of Brahms: "His fancy is lacking in melodic tide," and also, "Brahms' music has no profile; . . . by this remark I do not mean absolute censure, for, like Handel, one can have too much profile, too much nose and chin, and too little of the full glance of the eye."

I transcribe all this to show you the impression made upon his doubting contemporaries by this richly gifted composer.

IV

In op. 21 there are two sets of variations—one in D, on an original theme, the second in the same key, on a Hungarian song. They are both excellent preparatory studies for the more famous pair. In them we get the peculiar Brahms technic amply illustrated — for instance, the first variation of the opus. It begins with a characteristic figure in the bass, the harmonic extensions showing how ingeniously Brahms handled the arpeggio, avoiding a tone, accentuating another and gaining new color. There are some interesting variations in this set, No. 7, with its wide intervals; No. 9, another pedal bass effect with huge skips that look like yawning precipices, yet I do not particularly care for the set, although constant study of Brahms reveals new points of interest. The variations on a Hungarian song are even less fruitful in treatment, but will repay study.

When, however, we take up op. 24, variations and fugue on a theme by Handel, we begin to sense the extraordinary fertility of Brahms. The theme itself, in B flat, is a square-toed aria, and what Brahms does with it is most entertaining, ingenious and musicianly. From the very first variation, surely full of humor, we get a view of the possibilities of the variation form. I am not sure but that these variations are more ingenuous, less sophisticated, and contain less of the étude than the Paganini variations. As they are occasionally played I shall not go into detailed description of the difficulties, except to say that the entire twenty-five are alive with musical invention and a certain genial feeling, a geniality that eminently suits the ruddy-cheeked tune of Handel. There is the fifth variation in B flat minor, there is the fourth with its bass and treble dialogue, the fourteenth in double sixths and the energetic attack of the nineteenth are all noteworthy.

The fugue is a capital specimen of close treatment, yet in spirit very free. I do not begin to find it as dry as certain of the Beethoven fugues, and it is devilishly tricky.

The variations on the Paganini theme in A minor are frankly studies, but transcendental studies, only fit to be mentioned in company with Liszt's. Apparently the top-notch of virtuosity had been reached and there remained nothing for Brahms to do but let an astonishingly fantastic imagination loose and play pranks that would have caused Schumann to shout with admiration. The very first variation is a subtle compliment to Schumann's toccata, and the second, with the sixths in the left hand, is very trying for players with short-breathed fingers. In the third we get rolling rhythms that excite more than they lull. In the fourth Brahms asks too much of mortal man with a top trill on a chord, the left hand gambolling over the impossible. Then follow some octave studies the reverse of easy, especially the ninth in chords. The eleventh is a veritable toccata; the thirteenth one of the most brilliant and popular of the set. The fourteenth is terrible, exacting and long, for it closes the set. Brahms, to use a faded figure of speech piles Pelion upon Ossa in the coda.

The second book starts in with a tremendous and exciting study in double notes, and the sudden muscular contractions and expansion caused by alternations of double thirds and octaves is exhausting to anyone but a virtuoso. The tenth variation, marked Feroce, energico, exhibits skilful use of arpeggio forms, and the eleventh variation is simply baffling. In the next one we get a breathing spell, one of those green melodic oases in which Brahms proves to you how easy it is for a great, strong soul to be gentle and tender.

It may not be considered amiss here to take a passing glance at some of Brahms' daily studies for the piano. Naturally a man fond of solving abstruse technical problems, he could scarcely let pass the studies of other composers without considering them in varied aspects. So he has taken Chopin's tender, whispering study in F minor (op. 25), and broken it on the wheel of double sixths and thirds. It may be magnificent technic, but, as Rudyard Kipling would ask: Is it art? It is certainly legitimate experimenting, but I fancy not fit for publication. A flood of imitations have resulted, and in some cases Chopin has suffered exceedingly. Happily the extreme difficulty of the Brahms transcriptions will prevent them from ever becoming as popular as much of Chopin. They are written for a parterre of virtuosi.

The étude after Chopin is entertaining for the fingers, and of more educational value than Franz Bendel's treatment of sixths in his B flat minor study, the étude Heroique.

But what shall I say of the Weber rondo, the so-called perpetual movement, topsy-turvied by Brahms, and actually played by him in concert? It is very bewildering and finally laughable. As a left hand study in velocity it is supreme. He has subjected a presto by Bach to two rather drastic treatments, and the famous chaconne he arranged for the left hand alone. This latter has one good point, it can be played easily by both hands, and the immortal piece enjoyed, for with Bach, Brahms is reverent to a degree.

The fifty-one studies recently published are

the keyboard? Give us our cadenza, our big
triumphal entrance, and our brilliant fi
and we will endure a few bars from th
tra;" bars, let it be said, that a
allow the solo player to
recover his wind an
fingers.

But Brahms thought
critic and public; to hi
was the sonata form ampli
unless it had something to s
tongue between its burnished
not, however, imagine that the
few doleful chords to play. Th
culties enough, and of a trying
order. As for the seriousness of
we cannot deny that it is dark
especially in the orchestra, and full
strenuous, solid sincerity of the com
I cannot help thinking here of what H
wrote for the benefit of those who find Bra
too grave and earnest: —

> The same may be said of Æschylus and Dante, of Milton, of Wordsworth. . . . Music is an art of at least the same dignity as poetry or painting; it admits of similar distinctions, it appeals to similar faculties, and in it, also, the highest field is that occupied with the most serious issues. . . . If we are disposed to find fault with Brahms because the

little gold mines for the student of Brahms. They are more musical than Tausig's daily studies and also more normal. In them may be found all the norms of Brahms' technical figuration, the mixed rhythms, the curious extensions, the double notes in thirds and sixths, with all manner of ingenious fingering. Examine the fifth study, occupying but a page, and you will find the key to one of the most formidable difficulties in the Paganini studies. It is in broken octaves, arranged in scale fashion and taken at a rapid tempo. Various examples will be found of this figure. Then there are single finger exercises, skips, scales and interlocked octaves and chords. Both books are of the highest importance. Max Vogrich says that the title of the studies should be A Hospital for Disabled Virtuosi.

The twenty-one Hungarian dances were originally arranged for the piano and afterward transferred to the orchestra. They are so familiar in their orchestral garb that I need hardly allude to them except to say that some of them are not so well adapted for the piano. But there are a half dozen that will outlive all the Liszt rhapsodies, for Brahms has penetrated more deeply the Hungarian spirit, has caught color, swing, perfume, mad greater part of his music is grave and earnest, let us at least endeavor to realize how such a criticism would sound if it were directed against the Divina Commedia, or the Agamemnon, or Paradise Lost.

For Ehlert the D minor concerto was " his first crusade into the promised land of art." He furthermore finds it penetrating, rugged and unpleasant, but of " undisguised grandeur. . . . Its score represents the act of divorce between the pianist Brahms and the universal composer."

The first tutti covers all but five pages; but how entrancingly enters the opening subject! I find it simply captivating and without a trace of harshness. Of course if you will thump the piano like some pianists who believe that both Bach and Brahms are dry, pedantic music-worms, you cannot expect any response full of musical and intellectual charm. And let me say now that half the harm done to Bach and Brahms is that so successfully accomplished by pianists who fail to discern the exquisite musical quality of these composers. Give the public less arithmetic and more emotional and tonal variety, and presently you may find Bach and Brahms ending a programme instead of escorting a reluctant audience to its seat.

On page eleven of the concerto stands the second theme of the first movement in F. Show me anything lovelier, more suave, even in Mozart, and I will be surprised. It is the earnest and strict polyphonic treatment throughout and not any paucity of melodic material that irritates those that still believe music is made, like bonbons, to tickle the palate and soothe digestion. There is admirable logic in the working out section and plenty of finger, wrist and arm breaking technic. The last two pages — pages thirty-two and thirty-three — coming as they do, will force any strong musical man to exert himself.

The second movement, an adagio, gives us after Brahms the thinker, Brahms the poet. It is in the key of D and could only have been conceived by a man of the highest musical ideas and deep feeling. There is an episode on page thirty-six that gives the lie to the critics with strabismic hearing. It is in melody and harmony, simply golden. The rondo is in strict form, full of classic glee, and very effective, even in the old-fashioned piano sense. It demands enduring, honest fingers, and much breadth of style.

Properly speaking, the second piano concerto in B flat, op. 83, belongs to my so-called second manner of the composer. In it there is less of the philosophic brooding of the first concerto. It is more passionate, more fluent, more direct and more dramatic. It shows the same unerring grasp of construction; but there is, throughout, more of the musician of the world, less of the introspective and contemplative poet. It is brilliant — especially the passage work — for the piano. The enunciation of the first theme by the horn is memorable; beautiful, too, is the violoncello solo in the slow movement, while the Hungarian finale contains some of the most charming pages written for piano and orchestra. It is dashing and piquant, and the second theme is truly Magyar.

This concerto is always sure to be more popular than the first, with its Faust-like questionings. Brahms has dared to be worldly and less recondite for once.

V

It seems to me that the pièce de résistance of the Brahms piano music is the Paganini Variations; those famous, awesome, o'ertoppling, huge, fantastic, gargoylean variations erected, planned and superimposed by Brahms upon a characteristic theme of Paganini.

Brahms and Paganini! Was ever so strange a couple in harness? Caliban and Ariel, Jove and Puck. The stolid German, the vibratile Italian! Yet fantasy wins, even if brewed in a homely Teutonic kettle. Brahms has taken the little motif—a true fiddle motif—of Paganini, and tossed it ball-wise in the air, and while it spiral spins and bathes in the blue, he cogitates, and his thought is marvellously fine spun. Webs of gold and diamond spiders and the great round sun splashing about, and then deep divings into the bowels of the firmament and growlings and subterrene rumblings, and all the while the poor maigre Paganini, a mere palimpsest for the terrible old man of Hamburg, from whose pipe wreathed musical smoky metaphysics, and whose eyes are fixed on the Kantean categories.

These diabolical variations, the last word in the technical literature of the piano, are also vast spiritual problems. To play them requires fingers of steel, a heart of burning lava and the courage of a lion. You see, these variations are an obsession with me.

Now take up the Chopin Preludes, and the last, a separate one, op. 45, in the key of C sharp minor. It begins with an idea that Mendelssohn employs in his Song Without

Words in A minor, "Regret," I think, is the fanciful name given it by the publishers; but play until you come to the thirteenth bar, and, behold, you are landed in the middle of Brahms. I do not mean to say that Brahms copied Chopin, but the mood and its physical presentation are identical with some of the music of the later Brahms, the Brahms of the second period. The most curious part about this coincidence is that the ten bars that follow do not sound like Chopin, but Brahms — oh, so Brahmsian, that bitter-sweet lingering, that spiritual reverie in which the musical idea is gently propelled as if in some elusive dream. Then there are the extended chords, the shifting harmonic hues, the very bars are built up like Brahms. Of course Brahms would have been Brahms without Chopin; he really owes the Pole less than he owes Schumann, nevertheless here we are confronted with a startling similarity of theme and treatment.

I fancied that Bach anticipated everyone in modern music, but Chopin anticipating Brahms is almost in the nature of a delicate, ironical jest; yet it is not more singular than Beethoven anticipating Schumann and Chopin in the adagio of the sonata, op. 106, and in the arioso dolente of the sonata, op. 110.

There is nothing new under the sun, said some venerable polyphonic pundit, in omphalic contemplation on the banks of the Ganges, and music amply illustrates this eld saying.

But to op. 76, Clavierstücke von Johannes Brahms. This opus is divided into eight numbers, capriccios and intermezzi; for the composer disliked excessively giving his music set names, although it seems to me that with his intense Teutonism he might have followed Schumann's example and avoided the Italian nomenclature as much as possible.

Then again these little pieces are not always well named, for the rhapsodies are seldom rhapsodies in the conventional sense, and the intermezzi are, I suppose, intended to fill in, as the name indicates, some intermediate place; but as a matter of fact they do not, for they are often bunched together. It is to be supposed that Brahms attached some intellectual significance to these titles that is caviare to the general.

The first capriccio of op. 76 is in the key of F sharp minor, the brief, restless introductory suggesting, but rather faintly, Schumann. The principal melody is structurally in the style of Mendelssohn, but the harmonization and development of a sort that would have repelled the gentle Felix, who disliked anything bristling or forbidding. The mood-color is gloomy, even to despair. There is a ray of light in the diminished chord that preludes the return of the theme, which is treated in inversion — a characteristic trick of Brahms. Near the close the melody is sounded in quarter-noted chords and most resolutely, but soon melts away into vaporous figuration, the piece ending in the major, but without a ray of sunshine.

The second capriccio is the familiar one in B minor, played staccato throughout, and a piquant and almost agreeable piano composition. Do you know that I never hear it without being reminded of the fourth number in Schumann's Die Davidsbündler, which is also in B minor. It is as if Brahms took that syncopated page and built over it his capriccio, with its capricious staccati and ingenious harmonic changes. Of course the resemblance vanishes after the third bar; it is really more spiritual than actual.

Interesting it is to follow the permutations of the composer. On page nine there is a refreshing and perfectly sane modulation from E major to F, and the return to the subject is cleverly managed. The frisky yet somewhat saturnine character is maintained to the end, and the doubling up on page twelve is very effective. A genuine piano piece is this B minor capriccio.

We now come to the lovely A flat intermezzo, which occasionally strays in an uneasy fashion on the concert stage. A few pianists play this tender wreath of moonbeams and love, but either too slow or too fast. To play Brahms sentimentally is to slay Brahms; yet this charming intermezzo in A flat must not be taken too slow. It exhales an odor of purity, of peace, that is not quite untroubled, and nothing sweeter can be imagined than the dolce on the first page that follows a ritenuto and introduces a break in the melody. Its two pages are the two pages of a masterpiece. They give us Brahms at his best and in his most lovable mood.

The next intermezzo is more shy and more diffident. Marked allegretto grazioso, its graciousness is veiled by a hesitating reserve which further on becomes almost painful. Mark where the double notes begin, mark the progression and its dark downward inflection. But it is a beautiful bit of writing, with some of the characteristics of a nocturne, but full of questionings, full of enigmatic pain. Brahms, too, suffered severely from Weltschmerz.

The second book of op. 76 is a distinct advance in mastery of material, in the expression and realization of moods almost too recondite and remote. The C sharp minor capriccio which begins the book is more lengthy and more ambitious than any in the work. It is an agitated, passionate composition, driving through darkness and storm without relief, until a silent poco tranquillo is reached; but the point of repose is soon abandoned and the turmoil begins anew and the ending is full of gloom and fierceness. I catch Schumann in spots; for example, near the end of the second line on the second page, when a rank modulation stares you in the face, but with the eyes of Robert the Fantastic. The tempest-like character of the capriccio is marked. It is a true soul-storm in which the spirit, buffeted and drenched by the wind and wave of adversity, is almost subdued; but the harsh and haughty coda shows indomitable courage at the last. It is a powerful companion picture for Schumann's Aufschwung.

Then follow in the next intermezzo perfect calm, perfect repose of mind and body. In the slow moving triplets Brahms indicates those curves of quiet that enfold us when we are at one with ourselves, with nature. Indescribably lovely is the first page of this melancholy and reckless joy without a suspicion of the glittering embroidery of Liszt's virtuoso-like paraphrases. These dances of Brahms can be made to sound superbly if played by a pianist with temperament, above all a pianist who has in his veins Magyar blood.

I wish I had been in Leipsic in January, 1859, among the big-wigs of music and listened to the first performance of the D minor, the first piano concerto, played by its composer, Johannes Brahms. The Gewandhaus must have been disgusted by "the symphony with piano obbligato," as the critics called it; curiously enough, this work has set the pace for the modern concerto, of which Eugen d'Albert's two works in B minor and E major are extreme examples.

Yet carefully read the D minor concerto to-day, and much of its so-called obscurity vanishes. When I first heard the work played by Wilhelmine Claus, an excellent artist, I confess that, fresh from "Chopinism," this concerto sounded mournfully vague and uncertain. Its seriousness was, however, not its only drawback to popularity. "Where," asked a bewildered public, accustomed to the panderings of "pianism," "where are our trills, our scales, our runs all over the landscape of little gold mines for the student of Brahms. They are more musical than Tausig's daily studies and also more normal. In them may be found all the norms of Brahms' technical figuration, the mixed rhythms, the curious extensions, the double notes in thirds and sixths, with all manner of ingenious fingering. Examine the fifth study, occupying but a page, and you will find the key to one of the most formidable difficulties in the Paganini studies. It is in broken octaves, arranged in scale fashion and taken at a rapid tempo. Various examples will be found of this figure. Then there are single finger exercises, skips, scales and interlocked octaves and chords. Both books are of the highest importance. Max Vogrich says that the title of the studies should be A Hospital for Disabled Virtuosi.

The twenty-one Hungarian dances were originally arranged for the piano and afterward transferred to the orchestra. They are so familiar in their orchestral garb that I need hardly allude to them except to say that some of them are not so well adapted for the piano. But there are a half dozen that will outlive all the Liszt rhapsodies, for Brahms has penetrated more deeply the Hungarian spirit, has caught color, swing, perfume, mad greater part of his music is grave and earnest, let us at least endeavor to realize how such a criticism would sound if it were directed against the Divina Commedia, or the Agamemnon, or Paradise Lost.

For Ehlert the D minor concerto was "his first crusade into the promised land of art." He furthermore finds it penetrating, rugged and unpleasant, but of "undisguised grandeur. . . . Its score represents the act of divorce between the pianist Brahms and the universal composer."

The first tutti covers all but five pages; but how entrancingly enters the opening subject! I find it simply captivating and without a trace of harshness. Of course if you will thump the piano like some pianists who believe that both Bach and Brahms are dry, pedantic music-worms, you cannot expect any response full of musical and intellectual charm. And let me say now that half the harm done to Bach and Brahms is that so successfully accomplished by pianists who fail to discern the exquisite musical quality of these composers. Give the public less arithmetic and more emotional and tonal variety, and presently you may find Bach and Brahms ending a programme instead of escorting a reluctant audience to its seat.

the keyboard? Give us our cadenza, our big triumphal entrance, and our brilliant finale, and we will endure a few bars from the orchestra;" bars, let it be said, that about suffice to allow the solo player to settle in his seat, recover his wind and nerve and warm his fingers.

But Brahms thought differently from the critic and public; to him a piano concerto was the sonata form amplified, and the piano, unless it had something to say, must hold its tongue between its burnished ivory teeth. Do not, however, imagine that the pianist has a few doleful chords to play. There are difficulties enough, and of a trying and unusual order. As for the seriousness of the work we cannot deny that it is dark at times, especially in the orchestra, and full of the strenuous, solid sincerity of the composer. I cannot help thinking here of what Hadow wrote for the benefit of those who find Brahms too grave and earnest:—

The same may be said of Æschylus and Dante, of Milton, of Wordsworth. . . . Music is an art of at least the same dignity as poetry or painting; it admits of similar distinctions, it appeals to similar faculties, and in it, also, the highest field is that occupied with the most serious issues. . . . If we are disposed to find fault with Brahms because the

VI

Op. 116 is made up of two books of small pieces called Fantaisien and divided into capriccios and intermezzi, seven in all. A bold, restless capriccio, a presto in D minor, begins the set. Here is the later Brahms with a vengeance. Cross accents, harmonic cross-relations, and what Hadow calls organic unity in the emotional aspect with organic diversity in the choice of keys. Very daring, very difficult is this energetic composition. In the seventeenth bar we find the Hungarian creeping in, in the characteristic Brahms style, but it only peeps at you for a few bars and is lost in the hurly-burly of mixed rhythms and tonalities. The entire character of the piece is resolute, vigorous and powerful. It is finely developed both in the emotional and intellectual aspects.

The intermezzo in A minor which follows is lovely. In its native simplicity it is almost as noteworthy as the introduction to the Chopin Ballade in F major-A minor. Its sweet melancholy has the resigned quality that Maeterlinck speaks of when describing an old man who sits serenely in his chair and listens to the spiritual messages in the air;

sits humbly, peacefully, with sweetly folded hands, and awaits — awaits what? The tranquillity of this nocturne is unbroken even in the second part, where a whispering figure in the treble enlaces the theme. It is another of those vaporish mysteries, those shadowy forms seen at dusk near the gray, thin edges of forests. Whether from caprice or logic Brahms makes a chromatic détour of an entire line before the coda. It is as interesting as it is unusual. This intermezzo is for pure, pious souls, and it is not very young music. It contains an unusual sequence of chords of the seventh in two parts, the fifths being omitted.

Of different calibre is the capriccio in G minor. No. 3 of the set. Passionate, agitated and intensely moving is the first theme, and the second in E flat major recalls to Mr. Fuller-Maitland the style of the early piano sonatas. But there is freer modulation and more economy of material. Brahms was not a young man when he wrote this opus, yet for the most part it is astonishingly youthful and elastic. There is fire and caprice in this composition that make it extremely effective for the concert stage.

More remote, but exquisitely tender and intimate, is the intermezzo which begins the second book of op. 116. It is my favorite number, and its caressing accents set you dreaming. In the entire range of piano literature I cannot recall a more individual and more beautiful piece of music, and I am fully conscious that I am writing these words and all they implicate.

Solemnly the triolen are sung in the bass, but the treble phrase that follows is purely feminine and questioning. So slender are the outlines of this piece that they seem to wave and weave in the air. The pianissimi are almost too spiritual to translate into tone; and yet throughout, despite the stillness of the music, its rich quiet, there is no hint of the sensuous. The luxuriance of color is purely of the spirit — the spirit that broods over the mystery and beauty of life. Brahms' music is never sexless; but at times he seems to withdraw from the dust, the flesh-pots and the noise of life, and erects in his heart a temple wherein may be worshipped Beauty.

Of ineffable, haunting beauty is this intermezzo; and it is worth a wilderness of some sonatas and loudly trumpeted rhapsodies by men acclaimed of great reputation. The ending is benign.

The next intermezzo, in E minor, is, I confess, gnomic for me. It is marked andante con grazia ed intimissimo sentimento. It is in six-eight time, and built on phrases of two notes. Intimate, yes, but the intimacy is all on the side of the composer, for you must long pursue this cryptic bit of writing before you begin to unravel its complicated meanings. The composition is extremely original, extremely poetic; more like a sigh, a half-uttered complaint of a melancholy soul. To play it you must first be a poet, then a pianist.

The next intermezzo is really a minuet. It is in E, and finely differentiated from its companions of the volume.

A capriccio, also in D minor, closes this work. It is quite brilliant, and, oddly enough, contains a full-fledged bravoura passage, in the nature of a cadenza, and after the most approved modern manner. It, too, would be extremely effective in concert.

Op. 117, three intermezzi, leads off with a delicious cradle song, which I cannot quite agree with Max Vogrich, as being fit to lull to slumber a royal babe. Indeed, the child rocked to sleep by Brahms is not so aristocratic nor so delicate as the infant of the Chopin Berçeuse but it is just as precious, even if homelier. The character of the music is confessedly Scottish, and has for a motto

Herder's "Schlaf sanft, mein kind, schlaf sanft und schön!" The harmonies are thick, crowded, and the melody charmingly naïve and childlike. One might reasonably expect from Brahms the vision of some intellectual looking baby, its skull covered with metaphysical bumps and from its mouth issuing sounds of senile wisdom. But this is not the case, for it is a real lullaby we listen to, even if the second section is darker than one expects. The return of the subject with the octave in the upper voice is well managed, and the composition ends in cooing repose.

An intermezzo in B flat minor follows, and after playing and digesting it let me hear no more complaints about Brahms' style being "unpianistic." This number has been called Schumannish, but the comparison is a surface one. Its pages are truly Brahms, and very difficult it is to play in its insolent, airy ease.

The last intermezzo of the book in C sharp minor is of sterner stuff. Fuller-Maitland finds in it a suggestion of the finale of Brahms' third symphony. For me it is most exotic, and has a flavor of the Asiatic in its naked, monophonic, ballad-like measures. There is an evident narrative of sorrowful mien, and you encounter a curious refrain in A, as if one expostulated at the closing of

some gruesome statement. Of weighty import is this piece, and in it there is smothered irony and slightly veiled suffering, and in it there stalks an apparition of woe, of ennui. Page fourteen shows the hand of a master.

There are some who find this op. 117 a distinct gain over the previous work. I cannot truthfully say that I appreciate this criticism, for both volumes contain gems of the purest. Temperament has naturally its own preferences. I have broadly indicated my favorite numbers, and perhaps next year may discover new beauties in the compositions that now fail to make a strong personal appeal. Certain it is that no number should be slighted.

We now near the end, for only op. 118 and op. 119 remain to be considered. The first intermezzo in A minor of the former opus starts off in an exultant mood — a mood of joyful anticipation. In it you are glad to be alive, to breathe the tonic air, to be smothered in the sunshine. Tell me not in doleful numbers that Johannes Brahms cannot be optimistic, cannot hitch his wagon to a star, cannot fight fate. There is passionate intensity and swift motion in this intermezzo. While playing it you are billowed up by the consciousness of power and nobility of soul. The tonality is most diverting and varied.

The succeeding intermezzo is in F minor, and is andante. A very graciously pretty piano piece it is, and well within the grasp of a moderate technic. The melodic material is copious and rich, and the harmonies very grateful. For example, play the F sharp section and the following measures after the double bar in F sharp major; how genial, what resource in modulatory tactics, what appreciation of diversity in treatment!

A stirring and royal ballade in G minor follows. It is Brahms of the masculine gender, the warlike, impetuous recounter of brave deeds and harsh contest. Although the key coloring is gloomy, there is too much action, spirit and bravery in the ballade for gloom to perch long on the banners of the composer. A wonderful second subject in B interrupts the rush of the battle, which is soon resumed. Even its pauses are brilliant.

The fourth intermezzo in A flat has quite a savor of the rococo, with its gentle theme and response. Something of the Old World hovers in its rustling bars, the workmanship of which is very ingenious, especially in the management of the basses in the second part. There is a tiny current of agitation in this intermezzo, despite its delicacy of contour, its lightness of treatment.

No. 5 is a romance suffused with idyllic feeling. There is atmosphere and there is the heart quality, a quality lacking in most modern composers. A very grateful composition, simple and serene, is this romance.

E flat minor is the key of the last intermezzo of op. 118, and a trying composition it is, requiring nimble fingers, fleet fingers and a light, strong wrist. The idea reminds me of one of Brahms' earlier pieces, a mere kernel of a figure, which is expanded, amplified, broadened, deepened by the composer at will. It is full of fantastic poetry, and there is sweep and vision in the composition, which has a ring of dolour and is full of the sombreness of a sad, strong soul.

Op. 119 ends the Brahms music for the piano. The daily studies were doubtlessly written before. But the four pieces that comprise op. 119 may be said to be practically the last music for the instrument he loved so faithfully. There is no falling off in inspiration or workmanship. The idea and its expression are woven in one strand; there is much polishing of phrase and no lack of robustness.

The opening number is in B minor, an intermezzo, an adagio, and full of reverent, sedate music. Since Beethoven no one can

vie with Brahms in writing a slow, sober movement; one in which the man, moral, intellectual and physical, girds up his loins, conserves his forces and says his greatest and noblest. The sustained gravity, the profound feeling never mellows into the pathetic fallacy, and of the academic there is not a trace. This adagio is deeply moving.

The next intermezzo in E minor is of extreme loveliness; its poco agitato is the rustling of the leaves in the warm west wind, but they are flecked by the sunshine. A tremulous sensibility informs this andantino, and its bars are stamped by genius.

Fancy the gayest, blithest intermezzo, marked "joyfully" and you will hear the enchanting one in C. The theme is in the middle voice, and the elasticity, sweetness and freedom throughout are simply delightful. It is three pages of undefiled happiness, and only to be compared to that wonderful rhythmic study in A flat by Chopin, the supplementary study in the Fetis method. But Chopin is so sad and Brahms so merry, yet the general architectonic is not dissimilar.

A very Schumannish and vigorous rhapsodie in E flat closes the set, and is in all probability the last piano piece penned by the composer. In it Brahms returns to an early love, Schumann, and there are echoes of the march of the Davidsbündler in the beginning; no one but Brahms could have written the section in C minor or A flat. This rhapsodie is for me not as interesting as the one in G minor, but it is brilliant, and requires wrists of steel.

One who is better qualified to speak on the subject than myself, Mr. Max Vogrich, made the following suggestions as to the order in which these pieces may be played in concert. He writes: —

As the pianist cannot possibly play all twenty pieces in one concert, he must perforce undertake the painful task of selection. Every concert player knows that he can never win over his audience to sympathy, unless himself in fullest sympathy with the compositions which he performs. He will therefore play op. 116 through, and find in the very first number (Capriccio) an exquisite and highly effective piece, teeming with trying octave passages. If he will, he can sufficiently exhibit his technic — and his muscular fortitude — in this number. No. 2 (Intermezzo) and No. 3 (Capriccio) will strike him as less effective. But in No. 4 (Intermezzo) he will discover a gem of the first water, an adagio enchanting in its wondrous sonority — a study in tone. The two next following intermezzi, again, will afford less complete gratification by reason of their overcharged seriousness, also the Capriccio, conceived somewhat in the spirit of a study, and forming the close of op. 116. Quickly taking up op. 117 (Three Intermezzi), the player opens it at No. 1, a slumber song, but one excelling, in depth of feeling, delicacy and absorbedness of mood, anything ever produced in this class of poetry, Schumann's Träumerei excepted. It was penned by a king, and only a king should play it to lull to slumber a royal babe.

Would anyone be moved to tears by pure music, let him listen to the two succeeding intermezzi, especially the last, which is fitted to bring sentimental souls to the verge of despair. Brahms must have experienced much evil in his life! Finally, our growingly enthusiastic pianist reaches op. 118 and op. 119. And now he cannot tear himself away from the piano. No further thought of concert or audience disturbs him now; nor can he devote a thought to careful selection.

He further remarks that:

Since the days of the Fantasiestücke the Kinderscenen, the Kreisleriana and the Novelletten, that is, since more than half a century, the entire range of piano literature has had nothing to show which could be even remotely compared in intellectual import with these twenty pieces by Brahms.

Brahms has the individual voice, and in his piano music his almost Spartan simplicity sometimes unmasks the illusory quality of the instrument. Yet, I protest if you tell me that he does not write Klaviermässig. His technics are peculiar, but they make the piano sound beautiful; an eloquent tone is needed for Brahms, and your ten fingers must be as ten flexible voices. He never writes salon music, with its weak, vapid, affected mien. You needs must play much Chopin and Liszt, for too much Brahms makes the fingers sluggish, that is sluggish for the older and more rapid-fingered composers.

Touching on the content of his piano music we find much variety. He has felt the pessimism of his times, but his ideals were noble, and no man could prefer Fielding as an author and not be robust in temperament. He is often enigmatic and hard to decipher. Often and purposely he seems to encage himself in a hedge of formidable quickset, but once penetrate it and you find blooming the rarest flowers, whose perfume is delicious. To me this is the eternal puzzle; that Brahms, the master of ponderous learning, can yet be so tender, so innocent of soul, so fragile, so childlike. He must have valiantly protected his soul against earthly smudging to keep it so pure, so sweet to the very end. I know little of his life, except that he was modest to

gruffness, that he loved beer, the society of women and good cooking. Very material all these, but the man was nevertheless a great poet and a great musical thinker.

His piano music is gay, is marmoreal in its repose, is passionate, is humorous, is jolly, is sad, is depressing, is morbid, recondite, poetic, fantastic and severe. He pours into the elastic form of the sonata hot romantic passion, and in the loosest textured smaller pieces he can be as immovable as bronze, as plastic as clay. He is sometimes frozen by grief and submerged by thought, but he is ever fascinating, for he has something to say and knows how to say it in an individual way. Above all he is profoundly *human* and touches humanity at many contacts.

Let me conclude by quoting from that just critic of Brahms, Louis Ehlert: "It is characteristic of his nature that he was born in a Northern seaport, and that his father was a contrabassist. Sea air and basses, these are the ground elements of his music. Nowhere is there to be found a Southern luxuriance, amid which golden fruits smile upon every bough, nor that superabundance of blissful exuberance that spreads its fragrant breath over hill and dale. Now here, however, on the other hand, may there be met that

enervating self-absorption, renunciation of effort or Southern brooding submission to fate. . . . He neither dazzles nor does he conquer with an assault. Slowly but surely he wins all those hearts that demand from art not only that it shall excite, but also that it be filled with sacred fire and endowed with the lovely proportions of the beautiful."

Brahms is indeed an artist of the beautiful and nowhere is this better exemplified than in his piano music.

II

A MODERN MUSIC LORD

By the side of the Blue Sea is a great and green oak tree girt with a golden chain.
Day and night a marvellous and learned cat crawls around this oak.
When he crawls to the right he sings a song;
When he crawls to the left he tells a story.
It is there you must sit down and learn the understanding of Russian legends. . . .
There the spirit of Russia and the fantasy of our ancestors come to life again.

PHILIP HALE, after PUSHKIN.

I

THERE you have Russia: when the Russian is not singing songs, saturated with vodka or melancholy, he is spinning stories shot through with the fantastic, or grim with the pain and noise of life. In the European Concert his formidable bass tones make his neighbor's voice sound thin and piping. Napoleon prophesied that before the end of the century Europe would be either Republican or Cossack, and only a few years ago the Moscow

Gazette exultantly proclaimed that the "twentieth century belongs to us." By no means an anti-Slavophile in music, Henry Edward Krehbiel, as far back as 1885, uttered his warning, "'Ware the Muscovite!"

On the doorsill of the new century this old-young nation, if not master, is almost a determining factor in politics, art and literature. Tolstoy straddles the two hemispheres, having written one of the greatest novels of the century, and like some John Knox of the North, he thunders at our materialism and cries, "Ye of little faith, follow me, for I alone am following the true Christ Jesus, our Lord and Saviour!"

In politics Russia is the unknown quantity that fills the sleep of statesmen with restless dreams. In painting she is frankly imitative and too closely chained to the technical ideals of Paris; in sculpture the name of Antokolsky rivals Rodin, while in music she is a formidable foe of Germany.

One is almost tempted to write that much Russian music, certainly all modern Russian piano music comes from Frederic Chopin, if you did not remember Chopin's Slavic affiliations. Yet in a sense it is true. Chopin plays a big part in the harmonic scheme of all latter-day composers, Wagner not excepted

Not alone in the use of dispersed harmonies was he a pioneer, but in the employment of the chromatic scale, in the manipulation of mixed scales, the exotic scales savoring of Asiatic origin; Tschaïkowsky and Dvorák transferred to a broader canvas and subjected to a freer handling many of the Polish master's ideas. To deny to Chopin originality of themes, rhythms and harmonic invention would be pushing the story back one notch too many. Weber, Rossini, Grieg, Liszt, Dvorák, Glinka, indeed all the nationalists in music, might also be challenged critically on the score of originality.

If Russian music, the only organized musical speech of the nation, owes something to Chopin, Michael Glinka was unquestionably its father, for, like Weber, he lovingly plucked from the soil the native wild flowers and gave them a setting in his Ruslan and Life for the Czar. In his train and representing the old Russian school are Alexander Darjomisky and Alexander Seroff, while with "Neo-Russia" rudely blazoned on their banner, follow the names Cesar Cui, Rimski-Korsakoff, Borodin, Balakireff, Liadow, Glazounow, Stcherbatcheff, Arenski, Moussorgsky, Vladimir Stassoff and others. Outside of this pale and viewed with suspicious eyes stand the figures of Anton Rubinstein, who went to Germany and made music more Teutonic than Russian, and Piotor Ilyitch Tschaïkowsky, who, like Chopin had French blood in his veins, his mother being the descendant of a family of French emigrants.

It would be interesting to compare the cosmopolitanism of Tschaïkowsky and Ivan Turgenev. The great novelist, one of the greatest in Russia and France, was regarded by his contemporaries in the same fashion as the little masters regarded Tschaïkowsky. The big men like Gogol, Pushkin, Dostoïew sky were followed by scores of imitators, who wore their blouses untucked in their trousers. This was their symbol, and their watchword was "We are going to the people." It was a savage reaction against cosmopolitan influences, for Russia has successively suffered from the invasion of English, French and German ideas, customs, manners and even costumes. The rabid Slavophilist would have none of these; he hated Italian pictures, German philosophy and French literature.

Now Turgenev, loving Russia with a great love, yet exiled himself to study his country from afar. He saw her faults, he knew her rash, crass ignorance, her greed for foreign flattery, and he also felt her heartbeat. Not even Tolstoy is more drenched with affection for his land, not even Tolstoy wrote with more passion and pathos of his countrymen. But Turgenev lived in Paris. He was a great artist in words as well as ideas, and his artistry was so much damning evidence against him by the cultivators of the new Chauvinisme. What was form and finish to them that were "going to the people?" And so this noble man went to his grave discredited by his own people, and homage was accorded him by a foreign nation. It broke his heart, and the same rank nationalism certainly embittered the last days of Tschaïkowsky who, like Turgenev, practised his art passionately and persistently; and while the little men, Cui, Borodin and the rest, were theorizing and dabbling with nationalism, he, like a patient architect, reared his superb tonal edifices, built of the blood and brawn and brain of Russia, even though here and there the architecture revealed his Western European predilections.

In a word, Turgenev, Tschaïkowsky and Tolstoy were travelled men; they drank deeply at all the founts of modern poetry and philosophy, and each, without losing his native quality, expressed himself after the manner of his individual nature and experience, and how infinitely wider in range, depth and versatility are the utterances of these three masterful artists when compared with the narrow, provincial and parochial efforts of their belittlers! And then the three are great, not alone because of their nation; they are great personalities who would make tremble the ground of any other land.

Rubinstein alone seems to have slipped between the stools of race and religion. Born a Jew, raised a Christian, and of Polish origin, he played the piano like a god, and his compositions are never quite German, never quite Russian. He has been called the greatest pianist among the composers and the greatest composer among the pianists, yet has hardly received his just due.

Tschaïkowsky's life is the record of a simple, severe workingman of art. Clouded by an unfortunate and undoubted psychopathic temperament, he suffered greatly and shunned publicity, and was denied even the joys and comforts of a happy home. He died of cholera, but grave rumors circulated in St. Petersburg the day of his funeral; rumors that have never been quite proved false, and his sixth and last symphony is called by some the Suicide Symphony. A complete nervous breakdown resulted in

1877, and his entire existence was clouded by some secret sorrow, the origin of which we can dimly surmise, but need not investigate. A reticent man, a man of noble instincts, despite some curious pre-natal influences, of winning manners, honest as the tides, Tschaïkowsky went through his appointed days an apparition of art, and in its practice he lived and had his being.

He was born April 25, 1840, at Votinsk, in the Government of Viatka, in the Ural district. He died November 5, 1893, at St. Petersburg.

In May, 1891, Tschaïkowsky, at the invitation of Mr. Walter Damrosch, visited America and appeared in the series of festival concerts with which Carnegie Hall was opened. The composer conducted his third suite, his first piano concerto in B flat minor, the piano part taken by Adele Aus der Ohe, and two a capella choruses. He subsequently visited other cities, and was everywhere received with enthusiasm.

Tschaïkowsky's last notable public appearance was in the summer of 1893, when he conducted some of his own works at Oxford, and received the degree of Doctor of Music from the University.

II

In 1877 Tschaïkowsky became engaged to a lady whom he had met at the house of her relatives sixteen or seventeen years previously.

That he married her was known to few, and the musical world was surprised at the mention of a wife Antonina in the composer's will. She received an annuity, but not a liberal one, and perhaps that is the reason she disclosed the history of the curious courtship and marriage of Peter Ilyitch Tschaïkowsky.

He was constitutionally timid, and morbid in his dislike of women; his friends advised marriage. But he was nervous and moody and in no hurry, yet when Antonina told him that she intended to study at the Conservatory he said:

"It were better that you married!"

Peter hung fire, and Antonina, who had secretly loved him for four years, finally, after much church going and prayer vigils, determined to assist her modest friend—suitor he was not. She wrote him a letter proposing marriage, which he answered, and of all their acquaintance this seems to have been the happiest time. She must have had a good literary style, for Peter praised it, and finally called on her. He spoke of his gray hairs, but never mentioned hers, although she was at least thirty-four — he was seven years her senior. She answered that merely to sit near him and hear him talk or play was all she asked. Again he hesitated and begged for a day's grace. The next time he saw her he said he had never loved; that he was too old to love, but as she was the first woman he had ever met that had pleased him he would make a proposition. It was this: If a brotherly love and union would satisfy her ideal of mated life he would consent to a marriage. After this coy proposal the matter was debated in a perfectly calm manner, and as he left her he asked:

"Well?" She threw her arms about his neck, and he hastily fled.

After that he visited her during the afternoons, but avoided all attempts at tenderness, only kissed her hand, and even dispensed with the familiar "thou." In a week he begged for a month's leave of absence, as he had to finish his opera, Eugene Onegin. Madame Tschaïkowsky declared that it was "a composition dictated by love." Onegin is Tschaïkowsky, Tatjana is Antonina, and she furthermore said that all the operas he had written before or since meeting her were cold. The marriage occurred July 27, 1877, eleven days after Tschaïkowsky returned to Moscow.

The sequel of such an extraordinary wooing may be easily foreseen. Tschaïkowsky's morbidity increased, and he seems to have taken an intense dislike to his bride. Everything she did displeased him; he objected to her costumes, and one can hardly blame him, for at the tea table one evening she appeared in a light yellow gown, wearing a coral necklace! When he discovered the corals were imitation he burst from the room, crying: "How fine, my wife wears false corals!"

In six weeks Tschaïkowsky had enough of married life, and left for a Caucasian water cure; but it was really an excuse, as he went to visit his sister. She must have given him advice, for he returned to his wife; but after three weeks more, and in the middle of the month of November, he told her that he had a business trip to make. She went unsuspectingly with him to the railroad depot, where his courage almost forsook him, and he took his final leave of her, trembling like a drunken man. He embraced her several times, and finally pushed her away with the ejaculation:

"Now go; God be with you!" They never met again. She only partially explains the catastrophe by saying that outside influences were brought to bear on her husband. Averse to conjugal life, credulous as a child and extremely irritable, he was led to believe that matrimony would prove fatal to his development as a musician. There is no doubt that this was true; indeed for such a neurotic, erratic temperament marriage was little better than prussic acid. Antonina doubtlessly suffered much and understood Tschaïkowsky's peculiarities, yet she did not complain until after his death, and then only when she found that the bulk of his property had been left to his favorite nephew.

There is no need of further delving into the pathology of this case, which bears all the hall marks familiar to specialists in nervous diseases, but it is well to keep the fact in view, because of its important bearing on his music, some of which is truly pathological.

I once wrote of Tschaïkowsky that he said great things in a great manner. Now I sometimes feel that the manner often exceeds the matter; that his masterly manipulation of mediocre thematic material often leads us astray; yet, at his best, when idea and execution are firmly welded, this man is a great man; one who felt deeply, suffered and drank deeply at the acid spring of sorrow. Not as logical nor as profound a thinker as Brahms, he is more dramatic, more intense, and displays more surface emotion. You miss the mighty sullen and sluggish ground swells of feeling in Tschaïkowsky; but then he paints better than the Hamburg-Vienna composer; his brush is dipped in more glowing colors; his palette is more various in hues, while the barbaric swing of his music is usually tempered by European culture and restraint. Reticent in life, he overflows in his art. No composer except Schumann tells us so much of himself. Every piece of his work is signed, and often he does not hesitate to make the most astounding, the most alarming confessions.

He fulfilled in his music much that Rubinstein left unsaid. Rubinstein was a Teutonic mind Russianized; but, unlike Rubinstein, Tschaïkowsky, with all his Western culture, kept his skirts clear of Germany. Her science he had at his finger tips, but he preferred remaining Russian. His ardent musical temperament was strongly affected by France and Italy. He has certainly loved the luscious cantilena of Italy, and has worshipped at the strange shrine of Berlioz. Indeed

Berlioz and Liszt are his artistic sponsors; and the French strain in his blood must not be overlooked.

In his later years, as if his own clime had chilled his spirit, he solaced himself in Italy and Spain, a not incurious taste in a stern Northman. Despite his Western affiliation there is always some Asiatic lurking in Tschaïkowsky's scores. One can never be quite sure when the Calmuck — which is said to be skin deep in every Russian — will break forth. Gusts of unbridled passions, smelling of the rapine of Gogol's wild heroes of the Steppes, sweep across his pages, and sometimes the smell of blood is too much for us, unaccustomed as we are to such a high noon of rout, revelry and disorder.

He was a poet as well as a musician. He preached more treason against his government than did Pushkin, or those "cannons buried in flowers" of the Pole Chopin. His culture was many sided; he could paint the desperate loves of Romeo and Juliet, could master Hamlet, the doubting thinker and man of sensibility; could feel the pathetic pain of Francesca da Rimini, and proved that Lermontov was not the only Slav who understood Byron's Manfred; he set Tolstoy's serenade to barbaric Iberian tones, and wrote with tears at his heart that most moving song, Nur wer die Sehnsucht Kennt, a song that epitomizes Goethe's poem; and then only think of the F minor, the E minor and the B minor symphonies! What a wonderful man he was! and how his noble personality tops all the little masters of the Neo-Russian school!

Tschaïkowsky was one who felt many influences before he hewed for himself a clear cut, individual path. We continually see in him the ferment of the young East, rebelling, tugging against the restraining bonds of Occidental culture. But, like Turgenev, he chastened his art; he polished it, and gave us the cry, the song of the strange land in a worthy, artistic setting. His feeling for hues, as shown in his instrumentation, is wonderful. His orchestra fairly blazes at times. He is higher pitched in his color scheme than any of the moderns, with the exception of Richard Strauss; but while we get daring harmonic combinations, there are no unnatural unions of instruments; no forced marriages of reeds and brass; no artificial or high pitched voicing, nor are odd and archaic instruments employed. Indeed Tschaïkowsky uses sparingly the English horn. His orchestra is normal. His possible weakness is the flute, for which he had an enormous predilection. His imagination sometimes played him sinister tricks, such as the lugubrious valse in the Fifth Symphony and the stinging shower of pizzicati in the Fourth.

He was not a great symphonist like Brahms; he had not the sense of formal beauty, preferring instead to work in free fashion within the easy and loosely flowing lines of the overture-fantaisie. The roots of the form are not difficult to discover. The Liszt symphonic poem and its congeries were for Tschaïkowsky a point of departure. Dr. Dvorák was therefore in a sense correct when he declared to me that Tschaïkowsky was not as great a symphonist as a variationist.

He takes small, compact themes, nugget-like motives, which he subjects to the most daring and scrutinizing treatment. He polishes, expands, varies and develops his ideas in a marvellous manner, and if the form is often wavering the decoration is always gorgeous. Tschaïkowsky is seldom a landscape painter; he has not the open air naïveté of Dvorák, but his voice is a more cultivated one. He has touched many of the master minds of literature — Shakespeare, Dante, Goethe, Byron and Tolstoy, and is able to give in the most condensed, dramatic style his subjective impressions of their poems. He is first and last a dramatic poet. He delineates the human soul in the convulsions of love, hate, joy and fear; he is an unique master of rhythms and of the torrential dynamics that express primal emotions in the full flood. His music has not the babbling rivulets, the unclouded skies, the sweet and swirling shepherds and shepherdesses of Dvorák, but it is more psychologic. Give Tschaïkowsky one or two large human figures, give him a stirring situation, and then hark to the man as his dramatic impulse begins to play havoc. As well talk of form to Browning when Ottima and Seebold faced each other in the ghastly glare of the lightning in that guilty garden of old Italy!

Tschaïkowsky has more to say than any other Russian composer, and says it better. He is no mere music maker, as Rubinstein often is, writing respectable, uninspired routine stuff. He worked earnestly, tremendously. Hence we find in his music great intellectual energy, great dramatic power, ofttimes beauty of utterance, although he is less spontaneous than Rubinstein. He had not that master's native talent, but he cultivated his gifts with more assiduity. His style is not impeccable, and is seldom lofty, but he has plenty of melody, charming melody, and while he was not a seeker after the one precious word, the perfect phrase, yet his measures are more polished; show the effect of a keener and more rigorous criticism than Rubinstein's.

Tschaïkowsky is eclectic, and many cosmopolitan woofs run through the fabric of his music. Italy influenced, then Germany, then France, and in his latter day he let lightly fall the reins on the neck of his Pegasus, and was much given to joyously riding in the fabled country of ballet, pantomime and other delightful places.

He is eminently nervous, modern and intense; he felt deeply and suffered greatly; so his music is fibred with sorrow, and sometimes morbid and full of hectic passion. He is often feverishly unhealthy, and is never as sane as Brahms or Saint-Saëns. His gamut is not so wide as deep and troubled, and he has exquisite moments of madness. He can be heroic, tender, bizarre and hugely fierce. His music bites, and the ethical serenity of Beethoven he never attains; but of what weighty import are some of his scores; what passionate tumults, what defiance of the powers that be, what impotent titanic straining, what masses of tone he sends scurrying across his pain-riven canvases! The tragedy of a life is penned behind the bars of his music. Tschaïkowsky was out of joint with his surroundings; women delighted him not, and so he solaced himself with herculean labors — labors that made him the most interesting, but not the greatest composer of his day.

He had in a rare degree the gift of musical characterization; the power of telling in the orchestra a poetic story, and without the accessories of footlights, scenery, costumes or singers. Charles Lamb most certainly would not have admired him.

And Russia, how he loved her! That wonderful Russia which Turgenev loved and divined so perfectly. Listen to Turgenev; listen to the pessimistic side of the Russian:

" Sadness came over me and a kind of indifferent dreariness. And I was not sad and dreary simply because it was Russia I was flying over. No; the earth itself; this flat surface which lay spread out beneath me; the whole earthly globe, with its populations, multitudinous, feeble, crushed by want, grief and diseases, bound to a clod of pitiful dust; this brittle, rough crust, this shell over the fiery sands of our planet, overspread with the mildew we call the organic vegetable king-

dom; these human flies, a thousand times paltrier than flies, their dwellings glued together with filth, the pitiful traces of their tiny, monotonous bustle, of their comic struggle with the unchanging and inevitable — how revolting it all suddenly was to me! My heart turned slowly sick, and I could not bear to gaze longer on these trivial pictures, on this vulgar show. . . . Yes, I felt dreary, worse than dreary. Even pity I felt nothing of for my brother men; all feelings in me were merged in one, which I scarcely dare to name: A feeling of loathing, and stronger than all and more than all within me was the loathing — for myself."

Now turn from this Hamlet-mood and read The Beggar!

I was walking along the street. . . . I was stopped by a decrepit old beggar.

Bloodshot, tearful eyes, blue lips, coarse rags, festering wounds. . . . Oh, how hideously poverty had eaten into this miserable creature!

He held out to me a red, swollen, filthy hand. He groaned, he mumbled of help.

I began feeling in all my pockets. . . . No purse, no watch, not even a handkerchief. . . . I had taken nothing with me. And the beggar was still waiting, . . . and his outstretched hand feebly shook and trembled.

Confused, abashed, I warmly clasped the filthy, shaking hand. . . . "Don't be angry, brother; I have nothing, brother."

The beggar stared at me with his bloodshot eyes; his blue lips smiled, and he in his turn gripped my chilly fingers.

"What of it, brother?" he mumbled, "thanks for this too. That is a gift too, brother."

I knew that I, too, had received a gift from my brother.

Russia, a stripling with stout, straight limbs and white hair, is all fire, caprice, melancholy and revolt. Turgenev, more cosmopolitan, lighter in his touch than Tolstoy or Tschaïkowsky, is able to give us in these two prose poems the sadness and the big heart of the Slav, but in Tschaïkowsky we get the melancholy, the caprice, the fire and the revolt. If he be not the most Russian of composers, he is certainly the greatest composer of Russia!

III

Like Rubinstein, Tschaïkowsky became celebrated as a composer after he had written a little piano piece — a Chanson Sans Paroles, curiously enough in the same key as Rubinstein's melody in F. A Polish dance, as we

all know, lighted Scharwenka's torch of fame in this country. Tschaïkowsky has never since written so tender, so dainty a piece as this little song without words. An op. 2, it gave him a vogue in the salon that has sent many a shallow admirer to sorrow, for it may be said at the outset that his compositions for piano are not Klaviermässig, do not lie well for the flat keyboard.

Read the very first opus, the Russian Scherzo in B flat, and you encounter a style that is decidedly orchestral. Massive octave and chord work, with dangerous skips and a general disregard for the well-sounding. In nearly all of his piano music I find this striving for the expression of the idea at the expense of smooth delivery, and we who have outlived the technical opportunism of the school that shuddered at the placing of the thumb on a black key must of necessity defend this course; but I wish to say for the benefit of those who groan over Brahms that he is a veritable Chopin compared to Tschaïkowsky — a veritable Chopin in his feeling for the right word and the right mechanical placing of it. Tschaïkowsky's writing for piano is that of the composer for orchestra. He thinks orchestrally, and his position as a technician might be placed midway between Schumann and Liszt. Beethoven, employing the technics nearest at hand — the Clementi technics — writes more idiomatically for the instrument than this latter-day Russian master. Hence the general indifference to his music manifested by pianists; hence the rareness of his name on concert programmes, for the whole tribe of pianists is sheep-like in its aversion to a new pasture, and only after the leader has leaped the gap in the hedge does it timidly follow and sniff at novel herbage.

For teaching purposes the pedagogue encounters a genuine bar in Tschaïkowsky's smaller pieces. After a page of delightful and facile writing, a flock of double notes or a nasty patch of octaves appear, and sometimes the teacher is himself floored by the difficulties. You may count on one hand the popular piano compositions of a small genre — the song without words, a real serenata, if ever there was one, with a streak of dark pathos in the middle; the number called June, from the Seasons, in the key of G minor, a barcarolle hinting of Mendelssohn and a stepfather to Moriz Moszkowski's barcarolle; the theme and variations from op. 19, a scherzo in F from Souvenir de Hapsal, and the Album d'Enfants, op. 39.

I shall not consider in detail all the piano orchestral or lyric works of Tschaïkowsky, but only the typical ones, and, furthermore, I urge pianists who are clamoring for a novel repertory to study and search for themselves and not be deterred by the absence of stereotyped forms of passage work, for, while Tschaïkowsky is never a path-breaker in this respect, his piano music is not always cast in an acceptable mould.

I have mentioned op. 1, No. 1, as being a Scherzo à la Russe; the second number an Impromptu. The little scherzo in F from op. 2 is tricky and full of vitality.

It is not difficult. The second theme is very pretty. This op. 2 also contains "Ruines d'un Château," and the familiar song without words, op. 3 — you see, I am in deadly earnest and mean to give you the story to its bitter end — is the opera Voyevode. Op. 4 is Valse Caprice, for piano in A flat, very brilliant; op. 5, the piano Romance much played by Rubinstein; op. 6 is composed of six romances for voice; op. 7 is a piano Valse-Scherzo, also played by Rubinstein; op. 8, a Capriccio for piano in G flat; op. 9, three piano pieces—a Reverie, a Polka and a Mazourka; op. 10, two piano pieces—a Nocturne in B and a Humoresque;

op. 11, the famous string quartet, E flat, with its entrancing slow movement; op. 12, an opera rejoicing in the felicitous title of Snegourotschka, or La Fille de Neige, a lyric drama in three acts. It was damned by Russian critics. Op. 13 — at last we come to a symphony, the first in G minor, sometimes called A Winter's Journey. It has been played here.

The work took shape under Rubinstein's eyes and has an antiquated flavor. It was composed in 1868 when Tschaïkowsky taught at the St. Petersburg Conservatory. If it were not for the last movement, which has a smack of the Calmuck, and the modern instrumentation, I should say that Mendelssohn had more to do with this youthful composition than Rubinstein. There is the same saccharine volubility, the same saccharine cantabile and the same damnable fluency that characterizes the work of the feline Felix. Of the poet that penned those masterpieces, Francesca, Hamlet and Roméo et Juliette there is not the faintest spoor.

The symphony is monotonously in the key of G minor, with the exception of the adagio. It is called A Winter Journey, and the slush must have been ankle-deep. The first two movements are labelled, Winter Journey

Dreams and Foggy Landscape, which of course may mean anything or nothing. The Allegro tranquillo is smooth, even smug, and one entire phrase for the wood-wind occurs in the working-out section of the first movement of Rubinstein's D minor piano concerto. The adagio is well made but is not musically convincing, notwithstanding its dark, rustling introduction, and the pretty conversation between oboe and flute. When the 'celli take up the solo one feels as if something were being accomplished. The scherzo is a melancholy apology and the trio cheap. In the finale, noisy and barbaric, we get a taste of our Tschaïkowsky, despite the garishness of loosely built fabric. The work is promising but we miss the large sweep, the poetic, passionate intensity, the keen note of naturalism and the fine intellectual acidity which we look for in this great composer.

Oddly enough it was Tschaïkowsky's favorite as is evidenced by the following communication from Mr. E. Francis Hyde the president of the New York Philharmonic Society: "When Tschaïkowsky was in this country in the spring of 1891 I used frequently to see and converse with him about musical matters. One evening when he was at my house, I had taken from my library the scores of his second, third, fourth and fifth symphonies and narrated to him the times of their first production in this country, and the circumstances connected with their performance. I then asked him which one of all his symphonies he liked the best, naturally supposing he would mention one of those lying before us. To my surprise however, he replied that he liked his first symphony best of all. He said that it was the first expression of his feelings in a large composition of purely orchestral form, and he had a peculiar affection for his first born. He did not enter into any details regarding its subject-matter but he expressed a hope that it would soon be produced in this country."

Tschaïkowsky may have been indulging in a little sentimental cynicism. Op. 14 is an opera, Vakoula, The Smith, in three acts; op. 15 is the Ouverture Triomphale; op. 16 comprises six romances for voice with piano; op. 17 the second symphony in C minor and known as the Russian.

In it Tschaïkowsky begins to reveal his skill in orchestration, and the themes of the first movement are all strong; at least two of its movements are not symphonic in character.

The first allegro, the strongest, is very Russian in thematic quality. The entire movement is characterized by a bizarre freedom, even recklessness. But there can be no doubt about the skill of its maker. The fantastic Durchführungsatz and the melancholy beauty of the opening — and very Slavic theme — are intimations of the greater Tschaïkowsky who came later.

He omits the slow movement and marches us to the lilting rhythms of Raff and Gounod. The harmonies are more piquant, for the Russian wields a marvellous color brush. It is a clever episode, yet hardly weighty enough for symphonic treatment. For that matter neither is the banal march in Raff's Lenore symphony.

The scherzo that follows is in the Saint-Saëns style. It reveals plenty of spirit and there is the diabolic, riotous energy that pricks the nerves, yet never strikes fire in our souls. The entire work leaves one rather cold. The finale is very charming and the variation-making genius of the composer peeps out. The movement has the whirl and glow of some wild dance mood and over all Tschaïkowsky has cast the spell of his wondrous orchestration. In the work are potentialities that are realized in his later symphonic works. It is our beloved Tschaïkowsky but as yet in precipitation. In style immature, there is much groping after effects — effects which he used with such a sure touch in Hamlet and Francesca. Those piano staccato chords for the brass choir, a genuine mannerism, are already here, and his fondness for chromatic scales, contrapuntally used, may be noted. An interesting symphony.

Op. 18 is The Tempest, a fantaisie for orchestra I never remember hearing. It was first played here by Mr. Frank Van Der Stucken.

In op. 19 we come once more upon familiar piano land, six pieces, the last of which is the variations in F. These are built upon an original theme, simply harmonized, savoring of a Russian cantus firmus. The first three are not striking; the fourth, an allegro vivace, is original in treatment; the fifth, an andante amoroso in D flat, suggests Chopin; the sixth, very bold and full of imitations; the seventh, short and in the mode ecclesiastic; eighth, in D minor, is Schumannish; nine is a fascinating mazourka; number ten is in F minor, and tender; number eleven, Alla Schumann, is characteristic; the twelfth on a pedal point is Brahms in color, and the presto finale, made of a figure in sixteenths, is very brilliant.

These variations give us a taste of Tschaïkowsky's quality in a form at which he was never beaten except by Brahms. They have served as models for several composers of the younger generation.

Op. 20 is "Le Lac de Cygnes," a ballet in three acts, also unknown to us, but the title is a charming one; op. 21 is six pieces for piano, dedicated to Rubinstein, a prelude, fugue, impromptu, marche funèbre, mazourka and scherzo; op. 22 is the second string quartet, almost as famous as its predecessor, but, if more euphonious, is not marked by the rude Russian vigor and originality of op. 11; op. 23 is the first piano concerto in B flat minor, and here let us tarry before again plunging further in the thicket of twisting, octopus-like numerals.

This concerto, one of the most brilliant of works of its class written since Liszt, is quite as fragmentary as Xaver Scharwenka's concerto in the same key, but it is more massive, more symphonic in the sense of development, weight, power, color, but not of form. The piano part is not grateful, yet it has attracted the attention of such a pianist as Von Bülow, to whom it is dedicated.

The work is interesting and full of surprises. The march-like first theme in three-quarter time, the astounding brilliancy and fulness of the piano part makes this opening very imposing. The processional quality is broken by the enunciation of the theme in dotted notes, followed by a Lisztian cadenza, with a repetition later in the orchestra of the subject. Then come those truncated, slurred triplets for octaves in unison, which are so portentous, and with which Tschaïkowsky accomplishes so much; makes a mountain out of a mole hill. The flutes and clarinets indulge in imitations of this until the full choir joins in, and then in augmented tempo the piano repeats, and finally it all dies away in a cavernous manner, leaving you in doubt as to its meaning or what to expect. But the Poco meno mosso is delightful, albeit its halting, syncopated accent breeds pessimistic doubts, soon resolved in the flowing lyric measures which ensue. The shadow of Schumann hovers here on brooding wings; yet another theme presents itself in A flat for the muted violins, with a zephyr-like accompaniment from the piano. Pastoral is the effect and plangent the rippling arpeggi. This theme leads off in the development with the profile only of the triplets of the intermezzo preceding. The piano part bursts in with octaves, and is singularly rich and vigorous. This

reprise is full of learning and boldness of handling. I like the way the second theme reappears in B flat, although tonalities throughout are constantly shifting, and a harmonic haze, a blur of color, is often the only picture presented. The cadenza toward the close of the movement is more than three pages, and starts off in G flat, sounding suspiciously like the cadenza in Rubinstein's D minor concerto. The finale is very impressive. The second movement in D flat is exquisite; a melting, amorous nocturne, charged with the soft languors of a summer night in Russia. There is atmosphere and there is a beloved one being sung to. The prestissimo, a fairy scherzo, with dancing, delicate shapes, all disporting themselves to a vague valse tune that must have been born on the Danube. This section has been charged with being commonplace, but a clever concert master can with a pencil stroke give the bowing and rhythm the distinction it needs. Yes, Tschaïkowsky could be distractingly banal; he could add the two of loveliness to the two of vulgar and make the sum five instead of four.

The andantino semplice ends serenely; and the Allegro con fuoco which follows is Russian in its insistent, irritable hammering accent on the second beat of the bar. You can't help being carried away by the swing of it all, and the gay second subject relieves the drastic note at the beginning. All goes bravely, another subject appearing in Schumannish figuration. A dazzling movement this. Joseffy has altered the three pages of what he calls "Czerny unisons," and made the passage work more modern. The finale is thundering. This B flat minor concerto is, after all, Tschaïkowsky at his best on the piano. His melodies are sweet, for the most part sane, and there is a sense of restless power suffusing the entire composition. It will stand as one of his representative efforts.

Let us, O weary sister, O bored brother! take up our staff and again wander down this flower and fungi-dotted path of opus land. Op. 24 is our next number, and is the opera Eugene Oneguine, or Jewgeny Onegin. This was produced in St. Petersburg in 1879. It never proved a success, although transplanted in various countries. The mazourka and valse are familiar, and the polonaise in G has been arranged by Liszt for concert. It is sonorous and pompous, but for me rather empty. The lyric theme or trio is commonplace. Upon the opera as a whole I can pass no judgment, not having a score. Op. 25, more romances, six for voice; op. 26 is the Sérénade Mélancholique, for violin; op. 27, six romances for voice; op. 28, seven more; op. 29, the third symphony in D, a further step in power and variety in this form. The first movement is beautiful music. The introduction in D minor hardly presages the brilliant allegro with its clear cut and animated figure. This theme is martial in character, a charming second subject being announced by the oboes. The movement is concise and shows an increased mastery in form. The second movement, an alla tedesco in B flat, is sweet and quaint but hardly belongs to a symphony. The andante comes next, in D minor, it is short and elegiac and seems better suited to a suite. This idea is further intensified when you are confronted by a fourth movement in B minor and a finale in D. Five short movements do not make a symphony, for there is neither unity of thought nor tonality in the work; not so pregnant a composition as the second essay in the symphonic form.

Op. 30 is the third string quartet; op. 31 is the delightfully fresh Marche Slave for orchestra, which we have so often admired in the concert room; op. 32 brings us to the Tschaïkowsky we all feel is great, for it is the overture-fantaisie Francesca da Rimini, surcharged with the woe, the passion of the guilty pair who forgot that day to read their book, and so were slain, and were seen by Dante and the Shade of Virgil as their thin souls mounted in the spiral of sin and shame and in the stormy blasts of hell.

Not as often heard as the Romeo and Juliet, I nevertheless prefer it.

The Variations "Sur un air rococo," for 'cello and orchestra, op. 33, are excellently written, very ingenious and very difficult. Op. 34 is a scherzo-valse for violin and orchestra, and op. 35 the concerto in D for the same instrument. This has been heard here several times. It is romantic in feeling and a very interesting work, although by no means a masterpiece. Op. 36 is the fourth symphony in F minor, a symphony that only falls short of being as great as the fifth and sixth. It is like all of his symphonies; loosely put together but certainly more homogeneous than the last one. The first strong, sombre movement, the andantino di modo canzona, the scherzo pizzicato ostinato and the harsh and sweeping finale are all fine imaginative mood pictures. There is the melancholy, the droning lament, the feverish burliness of the Russian poet, the Russian peasant. The

scherzo is like a winged projectile. I shall speak of it again.

Op. 37, the only piano sonata of Tschaïkowsky, deserves resurrection. Its great length, fifty pages, has kept it in the libraries of pianists. Doubtless Karl Klindworth, to whom it is dedicated, plays it. Its opening is rudely vigorous, while a counter theme in G minor is a blending of Chopin and Mendelssohn; diffuseness follows, lack of cohesiveness being the gravest fault of the work. Here, as in most of the piano music, the thought is orchestral, and is writ large for orchestra. There is more simplicity in the E minor andante, and for a time the idiom is of the piano. The scherzo is the Tschaïkowsky of the merry mood, the waggish humor. He plays jokes throughout. The finale is all hammer and tongs. In a foot note the composer humbly suggests the correct use of the pedal, knowing that color, atmosphere, perspective are the very essentials of his piano music.

Six pieces for singing, as they call them, mark op. 38, the first being that devilish and rollicking and saturnine serenade of Don Juan in B minor, the text by Tolstoy. He sings to his love on the balcony. In the accents of a sinister Bravo he bids her from

behind the lattice, and there is fear and cynicism in this wonderful song, so full of fire and the melancholy of a foredoomed soul. A great song, and I shall never forget the night Edouard de Reszke sang it, with its growling piano ritornello. It sounded satanic.

Op. 39, to pick up the arithmetical thread, is the Piano Album for Children, and contains just two dozen little pieces fit for the soft fingers of babyhood, except where a stretch wanders in, that would tax an organist's thumb. Op. 40 is another collection of pieces, twelve in all, of medium difficulty. The Chanson Triste is familiar. Op. 41 is a Messe Russe for four voices, with organ and piano; op. 42 is for violin and piano, Souvenir d'un lieu cher; op. 43 is the first orchestral suite, and op. 44 the second concerto for piano and orchestra in G. This latter is dedicated to Nicolas Rubinstein, and the first time I heard it played in public was at the Philharmonic festival in 1892 at the Metropolitan Opera House, under Anton Seidl. Franz Rummel was the pianist, and even he, iron-handed as he was, had to make abundant cuts. The work, as I recollect it, is more closely knit in texture than the first of its form, and is more musical, more imaginative, if less brilliant and showy. It will figure on

the programmes of the twentieth century virtuoso. The pianists of to-day refer to it as a symphony with piano obbligato. It has since been played here by Siloti. The last movement is the most Russian, the second being an exquisite pastoral, while the opening allegro is rhythmically noble and broadly eloquent.

There is no uncertainty in the ring of its first theme, a theme of sonorous nobility and virile assertiveness. The man who made such a theme has the blood of musical giants in his veins, peradventure the blood is a bit crossed with a Calmuck strain. The first movement is admirably developed, and the orchestra and piano have it out hammer and tongs fashion, the piano getting the better of the situation, particularly in the tremendous cadenza set in a decidedly unconventional place in the movement. The second movement contains some lovely writing, and the piano has to concede to the violin a solo of charming interest, although it later takes its revenge by playing the melody harmonically amplified. But the work is much too long.

Op. 45 is the Capriccio Italien, for orchestra, of which I once wrote: It is Russian icicles melted into fantastic shapes by Neapolitan fire and terpsichorean fury. The

Russian loves to dream of the South. Even Heine wrote "Ein Fichtenbaum steht einsam." Philip Hale says that there are in it "passages needlessly and ineffectively vulgar." I accept his later judgment, for when I heard the piece I was color mad, and in those days I loved any color so it was red or purple. Op. 46, six vocal duos; op. 47, seven romances for voice and piano; op. 48, the serenade, for strings; op. 49, the Overture Solennelle, better known as "1812," an impossible and noisy overture; op. 50 is the lovely trio in A minor for piano and strings, written to commemorate the death of Nicolas Rubinstein, who was a near friend of Tschaïkowsky. It is a true elegy.

Op. 51 contains six piano pieces, valse, polka, minuetto, valse, romance and a valse sentimentale; op. 52 is another Russian mass for four voices, and op. 53 is the second suite for orchestra; op. 54 is another collection of songs, sixteen in number, and for youth; op. 55 is the third and most popular suite for orchestra, the theme and variations of which are heard nearly every season. The finale-polonaise of these is most brilliant; op. 56 is that tremendously difficult and long fantasie for piano and orchestra, written for Annette Essipoff, and played here by Julia Rivé-King.

I forget how many bars the cadenza contains, but it is so long that the audience is apt to forget there is an orchestra. Yet the themes are fresh, the execution in Tschaïkowsky's most virile vein, and if the cadenza were cut or omitted the fantasie would certainly be heard oftener, especially as the orchestra is so eloquent and entertaining. But who will play the surgeon?

IV

We are now in the very thick of the fight of the fierce battle waged by Tschaïkowsky for his ideals. To know the complexion of his soul you must study his orchestral works, and after his op. 57, six Lieder, comes the noble Manfred symphony, op. 58. If I had a spark of the true critic in my veins I would be able to give the dates of the performances of this — to use a banal expression — inspired work. But I am not a handy man at figures of any sort, and indeed barely remember the composition except as a magnificent picture in poignant tones, Manfred seeking forgetfulness of his lost Astarte in the mountains, the Witch of the Alps; and after a wonderful sketch of the Alps, with the piercing blue above the calm, a ranz des vaches not at all in the Rossinian manner, the death of Manfred, and the maddening tonal debaucheries in the hall of Arimanes. Here is our Tschaïkowsky at his top notch; the temper of the man showing out clear and poetic and dramatic to all extremes. The passion of life and its folly are proclaimed by a master pessimist who from his birth was sacrificed to those three dread sisters told of by De Quincey. A most moving and agitated tale, and one that almost shakes your belief in the universe. No joy of life here but a morbid brooding, a mood of doubt and darkness. There are desperate moments in the music, and Manfred's naked soul stands before us. The finale, with its sweeping melos, accompanied by the organ, is most melancholy, but not without a gleam of hope. Tschaïkowsky is a poet who sometimes prophesies.

Op. 59 is a Doumka, a rustic Russian scene for piano solo. Op. 60 consists of a dozen romances for voice, and op. 61 is the delightful fourth orchestral suite, Mozarteana, in which Tschaïkowsky testified in a lively manner to his love for Mozart. He has utilized the Ave Verum in a striking way, and not even Gounod himself was ever so saturated with the Mozartean feeling as the

Russian composer in this suite. It is a great favorite.

The Pezzo Capriccioso is numbered op. 62 and is for violoncello, with orchestral accompaniment. It is as wayward and Slavic as anything Tschaïkowsky ever wrote, ending in mid air, as is occasionally his wont. More songs comprise op. 63, and the opus that follows, 64, is the fifth symphony in E minor. It is the most Russian of all his symphonies and its basis is undoubtedly composed of folksongs. Its pregnant motto in the andante, which is intoned by the clarinets, is sombre, world weary, and in the allegro the theme, while livelier and evidently bucolic, is not without its sardonic tinge. The entire first movement is masterly in its management of the variation, the episodical matter, the various permutations in the Durchführung all being weighed to the note and every note a telling one. Not themes for a symphony in the classic sense, Dvorák thinks, yet not without power, if lacking in nobility and elevation of character. But what an impassioned romance the French horn sings in the second movement! It is the very apotheosis of a night of nightingales, soft and seldom footed dells, a soft moon and dreaming tree-leaves. Its tune sinks a shaft into your heart and hot from your heart comes a response; the horizon is low, heaven is near earth and carking life beyond, forgotten in the fringes and shadows. Some pages of perfect writing follow; the oboe and the horn in tender converse, and you can never forget those first six bars; all youth, all love is clamoring in them.

How that slow valse, with its lugubrious bassoon and its capering violins in the trio, affects one! A sorrowful jesting, quite in the Russian style. It is a country where the peasants tell a joke with the tears streaming down their faces and if the vodka is sufficiently fiery, will dance at a funeral. The clatter and swirl of the finale is deafening, the motto in the major key is sounded shrill, and through the movement there is noise and confusion, a hurly-burly of peasants thumping their wooden shoes and yelling like drunken maniacs. All the romance, all the world-weariness has fled to covert, and the composer is at his worst with the seven devils he has brought to his newly garnished mansion. It is this shocking want of taste that offends his warmest admirers, and his skill in painting revelries is more accentuated than Hogarth's. Certainly you can never affix the moral tag.

Tschaïkowsky is often possessed by these devils, and then the whole apparatus of his orchestra is shivered and shaken. His chromatic contrapuntal scales on the heavy brass, his middle voices never at peace, the whir and rush of the fiddles and the drumming and clash of cymbals are the outward evidence of the unquiet Calmuck man beneath the skin of Peter Ilyitch. That he can say obscure things I am willing to swear, and his neurotic energy is tremendous. This fifth symphony has its weak points; structurally it is not strong, and the substitution of the valse for the familiar scherzo is not defensible in the eyes of the formalists. But there are moments of pure beauty, and the mixing of hues, despite the Asiatic violence, is deft and to the ear bewildering and bewitching.

Just here I should like to make a digression and examine more fully the predecessor of the symphony in E minor, the fourth in F minor. In symmetry, beauty of musical ideas, suavity, indeed in general workmanship, it is not always the equal of the fifth symphonic work, but in one instance this may be qualified: The first movement is full of abounding passion, is more fluent in expression than the first allegro of the fifth symphony.

The theme in the introduction of the F minor symphony bears a strong resemblance to the opening of Schumann's B flat symphony, but not in rhythm. It is used in several movements later as a sort of leading motive or perhaps to give an impression of organic unity. The theme proper is romantic in the extreme and charged to the full with passion and suspense. The halting, syncopated phrases, the dramatic intensity, the whirl of colors, moods and situations are all characteristic.

The episode which follows the principal theme can hardly be called a theme; it is a bridge, a transition to the second subject. Tschaïkowsky can sometimes be very Gallic, for Gounod is suggested — a phrase from the tomb music in Roméo et Juliette — but is momentary. Musically this first movement is the best of the four, more naïve, full of abandon and blood-stirring episodes.

The second movement in B flat minor, andantino in modo di canzona, is a tender, sad little melody in eighth notes, embroidered by runs in the woodwind — Cossack counterpoint. It has a sense of remoteness and dreary resignation. It is uncompromisingly Slavic. It is said to be the actual transcription of a Russian bargeman's refrain. This is treated in a variant fashion — the second subsidiary in A flat being delivered by clarinets and fagottes, a middle part piu mosso in F, the whole concluding with the fagotte intoning the first melody. Sombre it is and not the equal in romantic beauty of the lulling horn solo in the slow movement of the E minor symphony.

The scherzo allegro in F, plucked by the string choir, is deficient in musical depth, but its novel workmanship fixes one's attention. It is called a pizzicato ostinato, although the pizzicati are not continuous. It is full of a grim sort of humor, and the trio for woodwind, oboes and fagottes is rollicking and pastoral. The third theme — smothered staccato chords for brass with sinister drum taps — is thoroughly original and reminds us of the entrance of Fortinbras in the composer's Hamlet. The working out is slim but clever.

The last movement in F is a triumph of constructive skill, for it is literally built on an unpretentious phrase of a measure and a half. It is all noisy, brilliant, interesting, but not of necessity symphonic. The main theme, almost interminably varied, is not new. It may be found in a baritone solo, Mozart's Escape from the Seraglio, and in a slightly transformed shape it lurks in the romanza of Schumann's Faschingschwank aus Wien. Tschaïkowsky's wonderful contrapuntal skill and piquancy of orchestration invest this finale with meaning.

Western ears are sometimes sadly tried by the uncouth harmonic progressions and by the savagery of the moods of this symphony. Symphony perhaps in the narrow meaning of the term it is not. A wordless music drama it could be better styled. All the keen, poignant feeling, the rapidity of incident, the cumulative horror of some mighty drama of the soul, with its changeful coloring and superb climax are here set forth and sung by the various instruments of the orchestra, which assumes the rôle of the personages in this unspoken tragedy.

How intensely eloquent in this form is Tschaïkowsky, and what a wondrous art it is that out of the windless air of the concert room can weave such epical sorrow, joy, love and madness!

Op. 65 brings us to six romances for voice and piano, and op. 66 the ballet of La Belle au Bois Dormant. Op. 67 is the Hamlet overture fantaisie, which evidently finds its form in Wagner's unsurpassable Eine Faust overture. It is remarkable in that it begins in A minor and closes in F minor. There seems to be little attempt to paint the conventional Hamlet mood, the mood of atrabiliary sluggishness and frenetic intellection, but rather hints of the bloody side of Shakespeare's purple melodrama. In it stalks the apparition, and the witching hour of midnight booms to the bitter end. There is the pathetic lunacy of Ophelia — a lovely theme limns her — and there is turmoil and fretting of spirit. At the close I am pleased to imagine the figure of Fortinbras thinly etched by staccato brass and the rest, that is silence to the noble spirit who o'ercrowed himself, is sounded in thunder that may be heard in the hollow hills. It is not Tschaïkowsky's most masterly effort in the form, but it is masterly withal, and its mastery is mixed with the alloy of the sensational.

Op. 68 is an opera in three acts, La Dame de Pique; op. 69, Yolande, opera in one act; op. 70, the lovely Souvenir de Florence, a sextuor for two violins, two altos and two 'celli. It is Tschaïkowsky at his happiest and he makes simple strings vibrate with more colors than the rainbow. Op. 71 is Casse-Noisette, a two-act ballet, a suite that has often been played here. It is dainty, piquant and bizarre. Op. 72 consists of eighteen pieces for piano solo, variously called Impromptu, Berçeuse, Tendres Reproches, Danse Caractéristique, Méditation, Mazurque pour Danser, Polacca de Concert, Dialogue, Un Poco di Schumann, Scherzo Fantaisie, Valse Bluette, L'Espiègle, Écho Rustique, Chant Élégiaque, Un Poco di Chopin, Valse à Cinqtemps, Passé Lointan and Scène Dansante, which last bears the sub-title of Invitation au Trepak.

These pieces are of value; many are graceful and suitable for the salon. The polacca and the scherzo are more pretentious and might be played in public. The imitations of Schumann and Chopin are clever. It must be confessed, however, that Tschaïkowsky often bundles the commonplace and the graceful and does not write agreeably for the piano. Rubinstein surpassed him in this respect. There is always a certain want of sympathy for the technical exigencies of the instrument and the suavely facile and the bristling difficult are often contiguous. There is no mistaking Tschaïkowsky's handiwork in these pieces, the longest of which, the scherzo, is twenty-one pages and quite trying. The most brilliant is the polacca.

It cannot be denied that the composer must have boiled numerous pots with his piano pieces, many of them are so trivial, so artificial and vapid. Op. 73 is six melodies for voice, and in these are four vocal romances without opus number. I have not said much about the songs, although they are Tschaïkowsky's richest lyric offerings. Some are redolent of the sentimentality of the salon, but there are a few that are masterpieces in miniature. Pourquoi, words by Heine, in German Warum sind denn die Rosen so Blass? is popular, not without justice, while Nur wer die Sehnsucht Kennt is fit to keep company with the best songs of Schubert, Schumann, Franz and Brahms. In intensity of feeling and in the repressed tragic note this song has few peers. It is a microcosm of the whole Romantic movement.

Among the unclassified works I find a cantata with Russian words, three choruses of the Russian Church, the choruses of Bortiansky, revised and annotated by Tschaïkowsky in nine volumes; an Ave Maria for mezzo soprano or baritone, with piano or organ accompaniment; Le Caprice D'Oksane, opera in four acts; Jeanne D'Arc, opera in four acts and six tableaux; Mazeppa, opera in three acts; La Tscharodeika, La Magicienne ou la Charmeuse, opera in four acts, and Hamlet — the overture I have already spoken of, — which consists of overture, melodrames, marches and entr'acts, regular music for the play. Then there is the Mouvement Perpétuel, from Weber's C major sonata, arranged for the left hand — Brahms has had an imitator — and an impromptu caprice for piano. Tschaïkowsky has also made a Manual of Harmony in Russian. The richness and variety of this composer's music is remarkable. Not coming into the world with any especially novel word to speak or doctrine to expound, he nevertheless has been gladly heard for his sincerity — a tremendous sincerity — and his passionate, almost crazy intensity. If you were to ask me his chief quality I should not speak of his scholarship, which is profound enough, nor of his charm, nor of the originality of his tunes, but upon his great, his overwhelming temperament — his almost savage, sensual, morbid, half mad musical temperament — I should insist, for it is his dominant note; it suffuses every bar he has written, and even overflows his most effortless production.

The history of the symphonic Ballade called Voyévode is interesting. In 1891 Tschaïkowsky gave the work a rehearsal and, not

has never been altered; the last movement is Tschaïkowsky at his greatest, but the other movements do not "hang" together; in a word, there is a lack of organic unity. Tschaïkowsky is never a formalist. He works more freely in the loosely built symphonic poem, the symphonic poem born of Berlioz, although fathered by Liszt. Yet we look for certain specific qualities in the symphonic form, and one of them is homogeneity.

Consider this last symphony. The opening allegro has for its chief subject a short phrase in B minor, a rather commonplace phrase, a phrase with an upward inflection, that you may find in Mendelssohn and a half dozen other classical writers. The accent is strong to harshness, and after the composer considers that he has sufficiently impressed it upon your memory the entrance of an episodical figure leads you captive to the second theme in D. Here is the romantic Russian for you! It is lovely, sensuous, suave. It is the composer in his most melting mood, and is the feminine complement to the abrupt masculinity of the first subject. Atop of it we soon get some dancing rhythms under a scale-like theme, and then the working out begins.

The second subject is first treated, and this is followed by an exposition of the first subject, and in thundering tones and with all the harmonic and rhythmic skill the composer knows how to employ so well. There is constant use of scales for contrapuntal purposes, and the basses shake the very firmament. It is the old Tschaïkowsky — sombre, dreary and savage. The mood does not last long. The sky lightens with a return of the cantabile, and then comes the schluss. This is wonderfully made and very effective. The movement ends peacefully. Its color throughout is beautiful, leaning toward the darker tints of the orchestral palette.

But the second and third movements are enigmas to me.

Raff introduced a gay march into a symphony, Beethoven a funeral march and Tschaïkowsky penned a lugubrious valse for his fifth symphonic work; but the second movement of this B minor symphony is in five-four time and sounds like a perverted valse, but one that could not be danced to unless you owned three legs. It is delightfully piquant music and the touch of Oriental color in the trio, or second part — for the movement is not a scherzo — produced by a pedal point on D is very felicitous. The third movement starts in with a Mendelssohnian figure in triplets and scherzo-like, but this soon merges into a march. The ingenuity displayed in scoring, the peculiar and recurring accent, which again suggests the East, helps the movement to escape the commonplace.

But why these two movements in a symphony? They are episodical, fragmentary and seem intended for a suite. Can it be possible that Tschaïkowsky has only given us a mosaic — has made a short rosary of numbers that bear no active relationship! As well believe this as strive to reconcile these four movements. Dr. Dvorák's words return with peculiar force after listening to this symphony. "Tschaïkowsky cannot write a symphony; he only makes suites."

Therefore the most tremendous surprise follows in the finale. Since the music of the march in the Eroica, since the mighty funeral music in Siegfried, there has been no such death music as this "adagio lamentoso," this astounding torso, which Michel Angelo would have understood and Dante wept over. It is the very apotheosis of mortality, and its gloomy accents, poignant melody and harmonic coloring make it one of the most impressive of contributions to mortuary music. It sings of the entombment of a nation, and is incomparably noble, dignified and unspeakably tender. It is only at the close that the rustling of the basses conveys a sinister shudder; the shudder of the Dies Iræ when the heavens shall be a fiery scroll and the sublime trump sound its summons to eternity.

No Richard Strauss realism is employed to describe the halting heart beats; no gasps in the woodwind to indicate the departing breath; no imitative figure to tell us that clods of earth are falling heavily on the invisible coffin; but the atmosphere of grief, immutable, eternal, hovers about like a huge black-winged angel.

The movement is the last word in the profoundly pessimistic philosophy which comes from the East to poison and embitter the religious hopes of the West. It has not the consolations of Nirvana, for that offers us a serene non-existence, an absorption into Neánt. Tschaïkowsky's music is a page torn from Ecclesiastes, it is the cosmos in crape. This movement will save the other three from oblivion. The scoring throughout is masterly.

Whether or not the composer had a premonition of his approaching death is a question I gladly leave to sentimental psychologists.

Again we must lament the death of the master. What might his ninth symphony not have been! He was slain in the very plenitude of his powers, at a time when to his glowing temperament was added a moderation born of generous cosmopolitan culture.

Little remains to be added. All who met Tschaïkowsky declare that he was a polished, charming man of the world; like all Russians, a good linguist, and many sided in his tastes. But not in his musical taste. He disliked Brahms heartily, and while Brahms appreciated his music, the Russian shrugged his shoulders, and frankly confessed that for him the Hamburg composer was a mere music-maker. In a conversation with Henry Holden Huss he praised Saint-Saëns, and then naïvely admitted that it was a pity an artist whose facture was so fine had so little original to say. He reverenced the classics, Mozart more than Beethoven, and had an enormous predilection for Berlioz, Liszt and Wagner. This was quite natural, and we find Rubinstein, with whom Tschaïkowsky studied, upbraiding him for his defection from German classic standards. Curiously enough, Wagner did not play such a part in Tschaïkowsky's music as one might imagine. The Russian's operas were made after old-fashioned models and, despite his lyric and dramatic talent, have never proved successful. He dramatically expressed himself best in the orchestra, and totally lacked Wagner's power of projecting dramatic images upon the stage.

As regards the suicide story, I can only repeat that while it has been officially denied, it has never been quite discredited. Kapellmeister Wallner of St. Petersburg, a relative by marriage of Tolstoy, and an intimate of Tschaïkowsky, told me that his nearest friends had the matter hushed up. He is supposed to have died of cholera after drinking a glass of unfiltered water, but his stomach was never subjected to chemical analysis. The fact that his mother died of the same malady lent color to the cholera story. It is all very sad.

Tschaïkowsky lived, was unhappy, composed and died, and he will be forgotten. Let us enjoy him while we may and until "all the daughters of music shall be brought low."

III

RICHARD STRAUSS AND NIETZSCHE

IN discussing Richard Strauss' symphonic poem, Also Sprach Zarathustra, its musical, technical, emotional and æsthetic significance must be considered, — if I may be allowed this rather careless grouping of categories. The work itself is fertile in arousing ideas of a widely divergent sort. It is difficult to speak of it without drifting into the dialectics of the Nietzsche school. It is as absolute music that it should be critically weighed, and that leads into the somewhat forbidding field of the nature of thematic material. Has Strauss, to put it briefly, a right, a precedent to express himself in music in a manner that sets at defiance the normal eight bar theme; that scorns euphony; that follows the curve of the poem or drama or thesis he is illustrating, just as Wagner followed the curve of his poetic text? The question is a fascinating one and a dangerous one, fascinating because of its complexity, and also because any argument that attempts to define the limits of absolute music is an argument that is dangerous.

Berlioz, Liszt and Wagner, three heroes of poetic realism, pushed realism to the verge of the ludicrous, according to their contemporaries. Liszt was especially singled out as the champion of making poems in music, making pictures in music, and giving no more clue to their meaning than the title. Liszt's three great disciples, Saint-Saëns, Tschaïkowsky and Richard Strauss, have dared more than their master. In Saint-Saëns we find a genial cleverness and a mastery of the decorative and more superficial side of music — all this allied to a charming fancy and great musicianship. Yet his stories deal only with the external aspects of his subject. Omphale bids Hercules spin, and the orchestra is straightway transformed into a huge wheel and hums as the giant stoops over the distaff. Death dances with rattling xylophonic bones; Phaeton circles about the Sun God, and we hear his curved chariot and fervent pace. But the psychology is absent. We learn little of the thoughts or feelings of these subjects, and indeed they have none, being mere fabled abstractions clothed in the pictorial counterpoint of the talented Frenchman.

In Tschaïkowsky, the lights are turned on more fiercely; his dramatic characterization is marvellous when one considers that the human element is absent from his mechanism. He employs only the orchestra, and across its tonal tapestry there flit the impassioned figures of Romeo and Juliet, the despairing apparition of Francesca da Rimini, and the stalking of Hamlet and Manfred, gloomy, revengeful, imperious, thinking and sorrowing men.

Tschaïkowsky went far, but Richard Strauss has dared to go further. He first individualized, and rather grotesquely, Don Juan, Til Eulenspiegel, Macbeth; but in Death and Apotheosis and in Also Sprach Zarathustra he has attempted almost the impossible; he has attempted the delineation of thought, not musical thought, but philosophical ideas in tone. He has disclaimed this attempt, but the fact nevertheless remains that the various divisions and subdivisions of his extraordinary work are attempts to seize not only certain elusive psychical states, but also to paint pure idea — the "Reine vernunft" of the metaphysicians. Of course he has failed, yet his failure marks a great step in the mastery over the indefiniteness of music. Strauss' German brain with its grasp of the essentials of philosophy, allied to a vigorous emotional nature and a will and imagination that stop at nothing, enabled him to throw into high relief his excited mental states. That these states took unusual melodic shapes, that there is the suggestion of abnormality, was to be expected; for Strauss has made a flight into a country in which it is almost madness to venture. He has, on his own opinions and purely by the aid of a powerful reasoning imagination, sought to give an emotional garb to pure abstractions. Ugliness was bound to result but it is characteristic ugliness. There is profound method in the madness of Strauss, and I beg his adverse critics to pause and consider his aims before entirely condemning him.

The object of music is neither to preach nor to philosophize, but the range of the art is vastly enlarged since the days of music of the decorative pattern type. Beethoven filled it with his overshadowing passion, and shall we say ethical philosophy? Schumann and the romanticists gave it color, glow and bizarre passion; Wagner moulded its forms into rare dramatic shapes, and Brahms has endeavored to fill the old classic bottles with the new wine of the romantics. All these men seemed to dare the impossible, according to their contemporaries, and now Strauss has shifted the string one peg higher; not only does he demand the fullest intensity of expression but he insists on the presence of pure idea, and when we consider the abstract nature of the first theme of Beethoven's fifth symphony, when we recall the passionate inflection of the opening measures of Tristan and Isolde, who shall dare criticise Strauss, who shall say to him, Thus far and no farther?

I

Richard Strauss said of his work when it was produced in Berlin, December, 1896: "I did not intend to write philosophical music or portray Nietzsche's great work musically. I meant to convey musically an idea of the development of the human racc from its origin, through the various phases of development, religious as well as scientific, up to Nietzsche's idea of the Uebermensch. The whole symphonic poem is intended as my homage to the genius of Nietzsche, which found its greatest exemplification in his book, Thus Spake Zarathustra."

For me the beginning is like Michel Angelo's Last Judgment, or the birth of a mighty planet; its close has the dreary quality of modern art, profoundly sad and enigmatic. There is no God for Strauss, there is no God in Tschaïkowsky's last symphony and there was no God for Nietzsche, no God but self.

You have Strauss' point of view, have you not? He disclaims making any attempt to set philosophy to tones; indeed Wagner's failure in Tristan and the Ring to ensnare Schopenhauer's metaphysic was sufficient warning for the younger man. The whole undertaking stands and falls upon the question: Is Also Sprach Zarathustra good music? I set aside now all considerations of orchestral technic — a technic that leaves Berlioz, Liszt and Wagner gaping aghast in the rear — and propose only the consideration of Strauss' thematic workmanship. Let it be at once conceded that he does not make beautiful music, that his melodies are unmelodious, even ugly, when subjected to the classic or romantic tests — call it classic and be done, for Schumann, Chopin, Liszt and Wagner are classics — and we have now further narrowed the argument to a question of the characteristic or veristic in melody making, and this is the crux of the situation.

Has Richard Strauss, then, made characteristic music, and how has its character conformed with his own dimly outlined programme — not Dr. Riemann's elaborate analytical scheme?

"I did not intend to write philosophical music," he said. Of course not; it were impossible; but some of the raw elements of philosophy are in the poem; keen, overwhelming logic, sincerity, orbic centrality, and hints of the microcosm and the macrocosm of music. Strauss set out to accomplish what has never before been accomplished in or out of the world, and he has failed, and the failure is glorious, so glorious that it will blind a generation before its glory is apprehended; so glorious that it blazes a new turn in the path made straight by Beethoven, Berlioz, Liszt, and Wagner!

Wagner sought the aid of other arts, and sang his Schopenhauer in gloomy tones; Strauss, relying on the sheer audacity of the instrumental army, chants of the cosmos, of the birth of atoms, of the religious loves, hates, works, doubts, joys and sorrows of the atom, would fain deluge us with an epitome of the world processes, and so has failed. But what colossal daring! What an imagination! What poetic invention!

The authors of Genesis, of the Book of Job, of the Songs of Solomon, the Apocalypse, the Iliad, the Sermon on the Mount, the Koran, the Divine Comedy, Don Quixote, Shakespeare's plays, Faust, the Ninth Symphony and Tristan, all rolled into one would have failed too, before such a stupendous task.

Now, perhaps we may reach a comparative estimate of the glory involved in Richard Strauss' half-mad, idealistic failure.

Putting aside Riemann as a hopelessly involved guide — a baleful ignis-fatuus in a midnight forest, — Strauss' poem impressed me, after three hearings, as the gigantic torso of an art work for the future. Euphony was hurled to the winds, the Addisonian ductility of Mozart, the Théophile Gautier coloring of Schumann, Chopin's delicate romanticism, all were scorned as not being truthful enough for the subject in hand, and the subject is not a pretty or a sentimental one. Strauss, with his almost superhuman mastery of all schools, could have written with ease in the manner of any of his predecessors, but, like a new Empedocles on Ætna, preferred to leap into the dark, or rather into the fiery crater of truth. In few bars did I discover an accent of insincerity, a making of music for the mere sake of music. He has leaped where Liszt feared to venture, and Strauss is Liszt's descendant as well as Wagner's. He cast aside all make-shifts, even the human voice, which is the human interest, and dared, with complicated virtuosity, to tell the truth — *his* truth, be it remembered — and so there is little likelihood of his being understood in this century.

It were madness to search for Nietzsche in Strauss — that is, in this score. It is un-Nietzsche music — Nietzsche who discarded Wagner for Bizet, Beethoven for Mozart. Schopenhauer, it may be remembered, laughed at Wagner the musician, played the flute and admired Rossini!

If Nietzsche, clothed in his most brilliant mind, had sat in the Metropolitan Opera House of New York City on the occasion of the first performance of his poem by the Boston Symphony Orchestra, December, 1897, he would probably have cried aloud: "I have pronounced laughter holy," and then laughed himself into the madhouse. Poor, unfortunate, marvellous Nietzsche! But it is Strauss mirroring his own moods after feeding full on Nietzsche, and we must be content to swallow his title, "Also Sprach Zarathustra," when in reality it is "Thus Spake Richard Strauss!"

The first theme — Zarathustra's, intoned by four trumpets — is solemnly prodigious; probably the dwellers in the rear world theme meant something to the composer. You see he has us on the hip; either accept his symbols or not; you have your choice, you believers in programme music; to me it was lugubriously shuddersome. I liked the beautiful A flat melody; it was almost a melody, and the yearning motive was tremendously exciting. In the section, Joys and Passions, the violins and 'celli sweep in mountainous curves of passion — never except in Wagner has this molten episode been equalled — and then the ground began to slip under my feet. I grasped at the misty shadows of the grave song, and the tortuous and wriggling five voice fugue in Science seemed like some loathsome, footless worm. The dance chapter is shrilly bacchanalian. It may be the Over-Man dancing, but no human ever trod on such scarlet tones.

And the waltz melody! why, it is as common as mud, and intentionally so, but it is treated with Promethean touches. When I reached the part called the Song of the

Night Wanderer, I renounced Bach, Beethoven and Brahms and became maddeningly intoxicated — not with joy, but with doubt, despair and defiance. Never shall I forget that screaming trumpet as it cut jaggedly across the baleful gloom! Sinister beyond compare was the atmosphere, and I could have cried aloud with Dante:

"Lo, this is Dis!"

I understood the divine laughter of Hell, and it surely was Dis that held its sides and cackled infernally! When we had reached the rim of eternity, "the under side of nothing," as Daudet would have said, there the "twelve strokes of the heavy, humming bell":

ONE!
O Man, take heed!
TWO!
What speaks the deep midnight?
THREE!
I have slept, I have slept —
FOUR!
I have awaked out of a deep dream: —
FIVE!
The world is deep,
SIX!
And deeper than the day thought.
SEVEN!
Deep is its woe —

EIGHT!
Joy, deeper still than heart sorrow:
NINE!
Woe speaks: Vanish!
TEN!
Yet all joy wants eternity—
ELEVEN!
Wants deep, deep eternity!
TWELVE!

Where is Hell-Breughel, painter, or Kapellmeister Kreisler, composer, after this weltering symphony of sin, sorrow and cruel passions? Their symbolism seems crude and childish, although Hoffman's musician was certainly a forerunner of Strauss.

There is one thing I cannot understand. If the Wagnerians and the Lisztianer threw overboard old forms in obedience to their masters, why can they not accept the logical outcome of their theories in Strauss? If you pitch form to the devil, there must be a devil to pitch it to. Strauss is the most modern of the devils, and to the old classical group he would be the reductio ad absurdum of the movement that began with Beethoven. Do you hear? Beethoven! To assert that his shoulders are not broad enough to wear the mantle of Liszt, I can only ask why? Liszt seems jejune when it comes to covering an orchestral canvas of the size of Strauss's. Strauss is his natural musical son, and the son has quite as much to say thematically as the father, while in the matter of brush brilliancy, massing of color, startling figure drawing — witness Don Juan and Til Eulenspiegel — and swift thinking, Strauss is easily the superior. He has not Wagner's genius; far from it; yet, as Otto Floersheim said: "Also Sprach Zarathustra" is "the greatest score penned by man." It is a cathedral in architectonic and is dangerously sublime, dangerously silly, with grotesque gargoyles, hideous flying abutments, exquisite traceries, fantastic arches half gothic, half infernal, huge and resounding spaces, gorgeous façades and heaven splitting spires. A mighty structure, and no more to be understood at one, two or a dozen visits than the Kölner Dom.

It lacks only simplicity of style; it is tropical, torrential, and in it there is the note of hysteria. It is complex with the diseased complexity of the age, and its strivings are the agonized strivings of a morbid Titan. Truthful? aye, horribly so, for it shows us the brain of a great man, overwrought by the vast emotional problems of his generation.

Also Sprach Zarathustra should be played once every season, and the audience be limited to poets, musicians and madmen. The latter, being Over-Men, would grasp its sad truths. And as I write I hear the key of B major and the key of C major and those three cryptic sinister Cs pizzicato at the close, and ask myself if, after all, Nietzsche and Strauss are not right, "Eternity's sought by all delight — eternity deep — by all delight."

II

Musically it is a symphonic poem of rather loose construction and as to outline; but rigorously logical in its presentment of thematic material, and in its magnificent weaving of the contrapuntal web. There is organic unity, and the strenuousness of the composer's ideas almost blind his hearers to their tenuity, and sometimes a squat ugliness. Strauss has confessed to not following a definite scheme, a precise presentation of the bacchantic philosophy of Nietzsche. Nietzsche was a lyrical rhapsodist, a literary artist first, perhaps a philosopher afterward. It is the lyric side of him that Strauss seeks to interpret. Simply as absolute music it is astounding enough — astounding in its scope, handling and execution. It is not as realistic as you imagine, not as realistic for instance as the Don Juan and Til Eulenspiegel. Strauss is here an idealist striving after the impossible, yet compassing the hem of grandeur, and often a conscious seeker after the abnormally ugly. Yet one hesitates to call his an abnormally evil brain. Abnormal it may be in its manifestation of eccentric power but it is not evil in its tendency, and a brain that can rear such a mighty tone structure is to be seriously dealt with.

As a mere matter of musical politics I do not care for programme music. Wagner and, before him, Beethoven, fixed its boundaries. Liszt, in his Faust symphony, and Wagner, in his Faust overture, read into pure music as much meaning as its framework could endure without calling in the aid of the sister arts. Strauss pushed realism to a frantic degree, giving us in his Death and Apotheosis the most minute memoranda. But in Also Sprach Zarathustra he has deserted surface imitations. The laughter of the convalescent, and the slow, creeping fugue betray his old tendencies. There is an uplifting roar in the opening that is really elemental. Those tremendous chords alone proclaim Strauss a man of genius, and their naked simplicity gives him fee simple to the heritage of Beethoven. But this grandeur is not maintained throughout.

The close is enigmatic, and the juggling with the tonality is fruitful of suspense, bewilderment. Yet it does not plunge the listener into the gloomy, abysmal gulf of Tschaïkowsky's last movement of the B minor symphony. It is not so simple nor yet so cosmical. Strauss has the grand manner at times, but he cannot maintain it as did Brahms in his Requiem, or Tschaïkowsky in his last symphonic work.

The narrative and declamatory style is often violently interrupted by passages of great descriptive power; the development of the themes seems coincidental with some programme in Strauss' mind and the contrapuntal ingenuity displayed is just short of the miraculous. There is a groaning and a travailing spirit, a restless, uneasy aspiring which is Faust-like, and suggests a close study of Eine Faust Overture, but there is more versatility of mood, more hysteria and more febrile agitation in the Strauss score. It is a sheaf of moods bound together with rare skill, and in the most cacophonous portions there is no suspicion of writing for the exposition of wilful eccentricity. There are reminiscences more in color than form of Tristan, of Walküre, Die Meistersinger, and once there was a suggestion of Gounod, but the composer's style is his own despite his Wagnerian affiliations.

Strauss is a man of rare and powerful imagination; the tentacles of his imagination are restlessly feeling and thrusting forward and grappling with material on most dangerous territory. The need of expression of definite modes of thought, of more definite modes of emotion, is a question that has perplexed every great composer. With such an apparatus as the modern orchestra — in Strauss's hands an eloquent, plastic and palpitating instrument — much may be ventured and, while the composer has not altogether succeeded — it is almost a superhuman task he sets himself to achieve — he has made us think seriously of a new trend in the art of discoursing music. Formalism is abandoned — Strauss moves by episodes; now furiously swift, now ponderously lethargic, and one is lost in amazement at the loftiness, the solidity and general massiveness of his structure. The man's scholarship is so profound, almost as profound as Brahms'; his genius for the orchestra so marked, his color and rhythmic sense so magnificently developed that the general effect of his rhetoric is perhaps too blazingly brilliant. He has more to say than Berlioz and says it better, is less magniloquent and more poetical than Liszt, is as clever as Saint-Saëns, but in thematic invention he is miles behind Wagner.

His melodies, it must be confessed, are not always remarkable or distinguished in quality, setting aside the question of ugliness altogether. But the melodic curve is big and passional. Strauss can be tender, dramatic, bizarre, poetic and humorous, but the noble art of simplicity he sadly lacks — for art it is. His themes in this poem are often simple; indeed the waltz is distinctly commonplace, but it is not the Doric, the bald simplicity of Beethoven. It is rather a brutal plainness of speech.

Strauss is too deadly in earnest to trifle or to condescend to ear tickling devices. The tremendous sincerity of the work will be its saving salt for many who violently disagree with the whole scheme. The work is scored for one piccoli-flute, three flutes (the third of which is interchangeable with a second piccolo), three oboes, one English horn, one E flat clarinet, two ordinary clarinets, one bass clarinet, three bassoons, one double bassoon, six horns, four trumpets, three trombones, two bass tubas, one pair of kettledrums, bass drum, cymbals, triangle, Glockenspiel, one low bell. two harps, the usual strings, and organ.

IV

THE GREATER CHOPIN

I

"AS-TU réfléchi combien nous sommes organisés pour le Malheur"? A fatal fleet of names sails before us evoked by Flaubert's pitiless and pitiful question in a letter addressed to George Sand. She could have answered for at least two — two names writ large in the book of fate opposite her own — Frederic Chopin and Alfred De Musset. Androgynous creature that she was, she filled her masculine maw with the most delicate bonnes bouches that chance vouchsafed her. Can't you see her, with the gaze of a sibyl, crunching such a genius as Chopin, he exhaling his melodious sigh as he expired? But this attrition of souls filled the world with art, for after all what was George Sand but a skilful literary midwife, who delivered men of genius and often devoured their souls after forcing from them in intolerable agony the most exquisite music? They sowed in sorrow, in sorrow they reaped.

It is not always meet and just that we exhibit to the gaze of an incurious world our intellectual Lares and Penates. There is something almost indecent in the way we rend our mental privacies, our heart sanctuaries. To the artist in prose, the temptation to be utterly subjective is chilled by the thought of the sacrifice. Hamlet-like, he may feel that wearing his heart on his sleeve will never compensate him for the holiness of solitude, no matter if the heart he dissects be of unusual color and splendor. Far happier is the tone poet. Addressing a selected audience, appealing to sensibilities firm and tastes exquisitely cultured, he may still remain secluded. His musical phrases are cryptic and even those who run fastest may not always read. The veil that hangs hazily about all great art works is the Tanit veil that obscures the holy of holies from the gaze of the rude, the blasphemous. The golden reticence of the music artist saves him from the mortifying misunderstandings of the worker in verse, and spares him the pang which must come from the nudity of the written word.

I have worshipped, and secretly, those artists in whose productions there is a savor of the strange. I loved Poe, although I seldom read him to-day. I thought Chopin the last word in music, until I heard Tristan and Isolde. I can never shake off my wonder for Flaubert's great chiselled art, and I would give a wilderness of Rubens for one Whistler. I know this may be a confession of æsthetic narrowness, but I never could bow down to overgrown reputations, nor does the merely big excite my nerves. In this matter I agree unreservedly with Mr. Finck. I would rather read Poe's Silence than all the essays of Macaulay, and can echo George Sand, who wrote that one tiny prelude of Chopin is worth all the trumpeting of Meyerbeer. It was in this spirit I approached Chopin years ago; it is in the same spirit I regard him to-day. But while my vantage ground has not perceptibly shifted, I descry a Chopin other than the melancholy dreamer I knew a decade ago. My glances are imprisoned by new and even more fascinating aspects of this extraordinary man and poet. It is of the greater Chopin I would speak; the Chopin not of yester-year, but the Chopin of to-morrow.

The old Chopin is gone for most of us. The barrel organ — not Mallarmé's organ, but that deadly parallel for pianists, the piano-organ, with its super-Janko technic —

now drives the D flat valse across its brassy gamut helter-skelter. The E flat nocturne is drummed by schoolgirls as a study in chord playing for the left hand, and the mazourkas — heaven protect us! — what have not these poor dances, with their sprightly rhythms, now wilted, been subjected to; with what strange oaths have they not been played? Alas! the Chopin romance is vanished. His studies follow those of the prosaic Clementi, and Du Maurier nabbed one of his impromptus for Trilby. Poor Chopin! devoured by those ravening wolves, the concert pianists, tortured by stupid pupils and smeared with the kisses of sentimentalists, well may you cry aloud from the heights of Parnassus, "Great Jove, deliver me from my music!"

What is left us in all this furious carnage, what undefiled in this continuous rape, this filching of a man's spiritual goods? Some few works unassailed, thanks to the master — some noble compositions whose sun-smitten summits are at once a consolation and an agony. To strive, to reach those wonderful peaks of music is granted but to the few. Even that bird of prey and pedals, the professional piano reciter, avoids a certain Chopin, not so much from instinctive reverence, but because of self-interest. He understands not, and also knows full well that his audiences do not. This hedges the new Chopin from cheap, vulgar commerce.

I have been criticised for asserting that in Chopin's later works may be found the germ of the entire modern harmonic scheme. It was not in the use of the chord of the tenth alone that Chopin was a path-breaker. Even in his first book of studies may be found a melodic and harmonic scheme, without which the whole modern apparatus of composition would not be as it is now. Does this sound daring? Come, put it to the test! That wonderful upward inflection which we look upon as Wagner's may be found in the G sharp minor part of the C minor study in opus 10. Look at it! Sift its significance and then revert to Isolde's Liebestod, or Wotan's entrance in the third act of Die Walküre. There is the nub of the entire system of modern emotional melody. Take all the études and what treasures do we not find? The lovely Fantaisie-polonaise, op. 61, has an introduction which is marvellous and which will sound new a century hence. There is a kernel of a figure that will surprise the Wagnerite who knows his Ring. I speak of a triplet figure in sixteenths in the introduction. It was the late Anton Seidl who first called my attention to the "Chopinisms" of the wonderful love-duet in the second act of Tristan. He said Wagner had laughed about the coloring. If Wagner is the oak tree, then Chopin is the acorn of the latter-day music.

What is this new Chopin I pretend to see? Or is it only as the soul in Browning's poem, All that I Know of a certain Star? Does my Chopin star dart now red, now blue, for me alone? Chopin left us four ballades and a fantaisie in F minor, which is a tremendous ballade, although not in the traditional ballade form. But it has unmistakably the narrative tone; it tells an overwhelmingly dramatic story. Yet of the four ballades, who dare play the first and second in G minor and A flat? They are hopelessly vulgarized. They have been butchered to make a concert goer's holiday. The G minor, full of dramatic fire and almost sensual expression, is a whirlwind; unsexed by women and womanish men, it is a byword, a reproach. Little wonder that Liszt shuddered when asked to listen to this abused piece. As for the A flat ballade, I can say nothing. Graceful, charming, it appeals even to the lovers of music-hall ditties. It, too, has been worried to death. The one in F has been spared for us. It is a thunderbolt in a bed of violets. Its tempest, scurrying and growling, is for the hand of the master. Let no mean disciple juggle with its vast elemental tones. Disaster dire will surely follow. And when the sky has cleared how divinely azure it is! The lilt of the breezes with thin thunder in the distance closes a page that is immortal.

When young I had no god but Beethoven, and all other gods were strange. To-day, hemmed in by the noise and dust of the daily traffic of life, I have a tiny sanctuary which I visit betimes. In it is the fourth ballade of Chopin, the one in the mode of F minor. It is a masterpiece in piano literature as the Mona Lisa and Madame Bovary are masterpieces in painting and prose. Its melody, which probes the very coverts of the soul, is haunting in its chromatic coloring, and then that fruitful pause in half notes, the prelude to the end! How it fires the imagination; how unlike the namby-pamby Chopin of the school-room and the critics!

The études are beyond the limit of this paper. I can only say that they are enormously misunderstood and misread. Studies in moods, as well as in mechanism, they are harnessed with the dull, unimaginative creatures of the conservatory curriculum, and so in the concert room we miss the flavor, the heroic freedom of the form. Who plays the C minor in the opus 25? Who ever gives us with true bravoura that dazzling drive of notes, the A minor, the second of the tonality in the same book? De Pachmann plays the study in thirds, but it is only a study, not a poem. When will these series of palpitating music pictures be played with all their range of emotional dynamics?

The impromptus are almost denied us. The fantaisie impromptu and the A flat, are they not commonplaces, seldom played beautifully? A greater Chopin is in the one in F sharp, the second. There is the true impromptu spirit, the wandering, vagrant mood, the restless outpouring of fancy. It is delicious. The G flat is practically undiscovered. Of the mazourkas, the impish, morbid, gay, sour, sweet little dances, I need not speak. They are a sealed book for most pianists; and if you have not the savor of the Slav in you you should not touch them. Yet Chopin has done some great things in this form. Think of the three or four in C sharp minor, the one in B flat minor, the curiously insistent one in B minor and that sad, funereal mazourka in A minor, the last composition Chopin put on paper. The singular idea of the last named, almost a fixed one, its hectic gayety and astounding gloom show us the sick brain of the dying man. But it is not upon these works I would dwell. The new, the larger Chopin will be known to posterity by the three great polonaises in F sharp minor, in A flat and the fantaisie polonaise. What a wealth of fantasy there is in opus 61! Its restless tonality, the marked beauty of the first theme, the almost vaporous treatment, the violent mood changes and the richness of the harmonies place this work among the elect. The F sharp minor polonaise and the two in E flat minor and C minor contain some strong, virile writing. They need men, not pianists, to play them.

Professor Frederick Niecks calls the F sharp minor polonaise "pathologic," and Stanislaw Przybyszewski, that curious, half-mad genius who, like Verlaine, has seen the inside of prisons, has written surprisingly of the polonaise; indeed, he is said to play it well, and has coupled the composer's name with Nietzsche's in his strange brochure, The Psychology of the Individual. To me the piece far surpasses in grandeur all of Chopin's polonaises, even the "Heroic," with its thunderous cannon and rattling of horses' hoofs.

It may be morbid, but it is also magnificent. The triplets in eighth notes in the introduction gradually work up to a climax of great power before the theme enters in single notes. Soon these are discarded for octaves and chords and do not occur again. The second subject in D flat is less drastic, less fantastic, and also less powerful. There is epical breadth in that beginning, and at each reiteration it grows bigger, more awful, until it overflows the limits of the keyboard. That strange intermezzo in A, which comes before the mazourka, is an enigma for most of us. It seems at first irrelevant, but its orchestral intent is manifest, and it leads to the D flat theme now transposed to C sharp minor and full of the blackest despair. If you play the thirty-second notes in octaves more color is obtained. The mazourka which follows tempted Liszt to extravagant panegyric. Its brace of notes, thirds and sixths, are lovely in accent and hue, but do not become languishing in your tempo, or the episode turns sugary and sentimental. With an almost ferocious burst the polonaise is reached, and again begins that elemental chant, which grows huger in rancorous woe until the bottom of the pit is reached, and then without a gleam of light the work ends in a coda, with mutterings like curses of the polonaise theme, and only in the very last bar comes the relief of a crackling and brilliant F sharp in octaves.

Pathologic in a sense it is, for it makes its primary appeal to the nerves, but it is wonderful music, though depressing. It hurts the very pulp of one's sensibilities, yet it is never sensational. I am reminded of Salvator Rosa's rugged, sullen and barbarous landscapes with a modern figure in the foreground, agitated, distracted, suicidal; in a word, something that paint and canvas can never suggest.

The nocturnes are sometimes beneath contempt. When I hear a Chopin nocturne played on the fiddle or 'cello I murmur complainingly as I listen, for it irresistibly reminds me of degraded beauty. There are exceptions. The vandals have vouchsafed us the one in C sharp minor, the gloomiest and grandest of Chopin's moody canvases. Its middle section is Beethovian in breadth. Ah! my friend, why do you take this piano composer for a weakling? Why give him over to the tough mercies of the Young Person? I would sentence to a vat of boiling oil, that is if I were the Sultan of Life, any woman who presumed to touch a note of

Chopin. They have decked the most virile spirit of the age in petticoats, and upon his head they have placed a Parisian bonnet. They murdered him while he was alive, and they have hacked and cut at him since his death. If women must play the piano let them stick to Bach and Beethoven. They cannot hurt those gentlemen with their seductions and blandishments, their amblings and jiggings. There are several other nocturnes that will never appeal to hoi polloi. The noble one in C minor, the fruity one in B and the one in E, form a triad of matchless music. They are not popular. The wonder-child that came to us through the pink gates of the dawn and was rocked to rhythmic dreams in the berçeuse has grown to be a brat of horrid mien and muscular proportions. I will have none of it. Its banal visage is cherished in conservatories. Long may it howl, but not for me!

The scherzi, the preludes, you cry! Ah! at last we are getting upon solid ground. The twenty-five preludes alone would make good Chopin's claim to immortality. Such range, such vision, such humanity! All shades of feeling are divined, all depths and altitudes of passion explored. If all Chopin, all music, were to be destroyed, I should plead for the preludes. The cameo stillness of some of them is as soft-spoken sentences in a cloister. Religious truly, but these appeal less to me than those thunder-riven visions in D minor, in B flat minor, in F minor, in E flat minor. Surpassingly sweet is the elegiac prelude in B flat. It is greater than any of the Chopin nocturnes. Number two, with its almost brutal quality and enigmatic beginning, is for a rainy day — a day when the soul is racked by doubts and defeats. It is shuddersome and sinister. About it hovers the grisly something which we all fear in the dark but dare not define. A ray of sunshine, but a sun that slants in the west, is the prelude in G. Why detail these marvels in miniature, these great and cunningly wrought thoughts ?

The embroideries of the barcarolle — a more fully developed and dramatic nocturne — and the bolero are both more Polish than Italian or Spanish. The fantaisie, opus 49, is considered by many to be Chopin's most perfect work. The grave, march-like introduction, the climbing and insistent arpeggio figures in triplets, the great song in F minor, followed by the beautiful episode in double notes and the climax of amazing power and almost brutality, give us glimpses of the new

Chopin. There is development, but only of tonality — if such may be called development — and the lento sostenuto is curt and very sweet. The end is impressive. The entire composition is larger in scope, its phrases fuller breathed, and there is a massiveness absent from much of the master's music. To my own way of thinking this fantaisie, with the F sharp minor polonaise, the F minor ballade, the C sharp minor and B minor scherzi, the D minor prelude, the sonatas in B flat minor and B minor, and the C minor study (opus 25), are Chopin at the top of his powers.

II

Frederic Chopin bequeathed to the world six solo scherzi. The four that comprise a group are opus 20, in B minor, published February, 1835; opus 31, in B flat minor, published December, 1837; opus 39, in C sharp minor, published October, 1840, and opus 54, in E major, published December, 1843. The other two are to be found in his second sonata, opus 35, and his third sonata, opus 58. They are in the respective keys of E flat minor and E flat major. These six compositions are the finest evidences of Chopin's originality, variety, power and delicacy. The scherzo is not his invention — Beethoven and Mendelssohn anticipated him — but he took the form, remodelled and filled it with a surprisingly novel content, although not altering its three-four measure. We feel the humor of the Beethoven scherzo, its swing, robustness and at times rude jollity. In Mendelssohn one enjoys the lightness, velocity and finish of his scherzando moods. They contain, strictly speaking, more of the truer scherzo idea than Chopin's. Mendelssohn's delicate sentiment of joyousness came from the early Italian masters of the piano. Rossini voiced this when he said, after hearing a capriccio of Felix the Feminine, "Ça sent de Scarlatti." Yet the Mendelssohn piano pieces of this character are finely considered efforts, full of a certain gracious life and a surface skimming of sentiment, like the curved flight of a thin bird over shallow waters.

But we enter a terrible and a beautiful domain in the Chopin scherzi. Two only have the lightness of touch, clarity of atmosphere and sweet gayety of the veritable scherzo. The other four are fierce, grave, sardonic, demoniacal, ironic, passionate, fiery, hysterical and most melancholy. In some the moods are almost pathologic; in some enigmatic; in all, the moods are magical. The scherzo in E, opus 54, can be described by no better or more commonplace a word than delightful. It is delightful, sunny music, and its swiftness, directness and sweep are compelling. The five preluding bars of half notes, unisono, at once strike the keynote of optimism and sweet faith. What follows is the ruffling of the tree-tops by warm south winds. The upward little flight in E, beginning at the seventeenth bar and in major thirds and fourths, has been boldly utilized by Saint-Saëns in the scherzo of his G minor piano concerto. The fanciful embroidery of the single finger passages is not opaque as in other of this master's compositions. A sparkling, bubbling clarity, freedom, freshness, characterizes this scherzo so seldom heard in our concert rooms. In emotional content it is not deep; it lies well within the categories of the elegant and the capricious. It contains on its fourth page an episode in E which at first blush suggests the theme of the valse in A flat, opus 42, with its interminglement of duple and triple rhythms. The piu lento further on, in C sharp minor, has little sadness. It is but the blur of a passing cloud that shadows with its fleecy edges the wind-swept moorland. This scherzo in E is emphatically a mood of joyousness, as joyous as the witty, sensitive Pole ever allowed himself to be. Its coda is not so forceful as the usual Chopin coda, and there is a dazzling flutter of silvery scale at the end. It is a charming work. Closely allied to it in general sentiment is the E flat scherzo in the B minor sonata. It is largely arabesque and its ornamentation is genial, though not ingenious. To me this scherzo savors somewhat of Weber. It might go on forever. The resolution is not intellectual — is purely one of tonality. The thought is tenuous; it is a light, highly embroidered relief after the first movement of the sonata. The trio in B is not particularly noteworthy. Truly a salon scherzo and challenges Mendelssohn on his native heath. It must be considered as an intermezzo and also as a prelude to the lyric measures of the beautiful largo that follows.

We get on firm and familiar footing when the first page of the B flat minor scherzo is opened. Who has not heard with awe those arched questioning triplets which Chopin could never get his pupils to play sufficiently tombé? "It must be a charnel house," he told De Lenz. These vaulted phrases have become banal. Alas! this scherzo, like the lovely A flat ballade, has been done to a cruel death. Yet how fresh, how vigorous, how abounding with sweetness and light when it falls from the fingers of a master! It is a Byronic poem, "so tender, so bold, so as full of love as of scorn," to quote Schumann. Has Chopin ever penned a more delicious song than the one in D flat, with its straying over the borderlands of G flat? It is the high noon of love, life and happiness; the dark bud of the introduction has burst into a perfect flowering, and what miracles of scent, color, shape we seize! The section in A has the quality of great art — great, questioning, but sane, noble art. It is serious to severity, and yet how penetrating in perfume!

The excursion in C sharp minor is an awakening of the wondering dream, but it is balanced; it is healthy. No suggestion of the pallid morbidities of the other Chopin. And how supremely welded is the style with the subject! What masterly writing and it lies in the very heart of the piano! A hundred generations may not improve on these pages. Then, fearful that he has dwelt too long upon the idea, Chopin breaks away into the key of E, and one of those bursts into clear sky follows. After the repetition comes the working-out section, and, while ingenious and effective, it is always in the development that he is at his weakest. The Olympian aloofness of Beethoven, Chopin had not. He cannot survey his material from all points. He is a great composer, but he is also a great pianist. He nursed his themes with wonderful constructive frugality; the instrument often checked his imagination. There is a logic in this exposition, but it is piano logic and not always music logic. A certain straining after brilliancy, a falling off in the spontaneous urge of the early pages force us to feel happy when the first triplet figure returns. The coda is brilliantly strong. This scherzo will remain the favored one. It is not cryptic and repellent like the two in B minor and C sharp minor, and is a perennial joy to pupil and public alike.

We now trench upon a sacred and not often explored territory of the Chopin music. The scherzo in E flat minor is one of the most powerful of the six. To play it effectively one needs breadth of style, a heroic spirit and fingers and wrists of steel. The tremendous crescendo in one bar taxes the strength of most pianists. The composition has something elemental about it. It is true storm music, and the whistling of the wind in the chromatic successions of chords of the sixth has an eerie effect on one's nerves. None of the Chopin scherzi stir me as this one. There is menacing gloom in the second bar, and the rush and grandeur of the movement take my breath away. The blissful song in G flat is not uninterrupted bliss. There is a threatening undercurrent, as if the howling tempest might return; it does, and how originally Chopin manages this! The descending octaves, which seem to carry us to the mouth of hell, are burst in upon by the first stormy theme, and again we are madly projected through space, a victim of the elements. Defiance, satanic pride, the majesty of the microcosm, a spiritual challenge to fate are all here. The lulling, lovely lines of the piu lento steal in again and the curtain rings down on a great picture of passion and pain.

Chopin's first scherzo in B minor bears an early opus number. It is his twentieth work — the most sombre, yet the most shrill and hysterical of the scherzi. It is in his most ironic, yet most reckless, vein; Chopin throwing himself to the very winds of remorse. A terrible mood, a Manfred mood, a torturing mood. A soul-shriek from the first chord to the last, with one dream inclosed within its gates of brass, it reminds one of the struggles of an imprisoned soul beating with wounded palms its prison door. It is the unhappiest, the most riotous of Chopin's works and suffers from prolixity. Its keynote is too tense for the da capos marked by the composer, and unsuited for latter-day taste. Some virtuosi play this scherzo without the repeats, and the piece gains greatly. It is so harsh, so drastic, that the wondrous melody in B, with its lapping, lilting tenths — "the sweet slumber of the moonlight on the hills" — after the tragic strain, comes like a benediction. This scherzo has almost had a special message. Chopin, like Robert Louis Stevenson, was afflicted with weak health, was slender of frame, but his spirit was brave as the lion's. Both men could write terrible things, even though they could not compass them. The sense of impotence, of stifled longings, fills this scherzo with inarticulate moans and bewailings. What a life tragedy is the opus 20!

The arabesque-like figure after the eight bar introduction — muted bars some of them, as was Chopin's wont — has a certain spiritual likeness to the principal figure in the C sharp minor fantaisie-impromptu. But instead of the ductile triplets, as in the bass of the impromptu, we divide the figure in the scherzo between the two hands, and the harshness of the mood is emphasized by the anticipatory chord in the left hand. The vitality of the first page of this scherzo is marvellous. The questioning chords at the close of the section are as imaginative as any passages Chopin ever wrote. The half notes E and the up-leaping appogiatura are also evidences of his originality in minor details. These occur just before the modulation into the lyric theme in B and with a slight change just at the dash into the coda. The second section, an agitato, contains some knotty harmonic problems. But they must be skimmed over at tempestuous speed, else cacophony. Bold here is Chopin to excess, as if his spirit would knock at the very gate of heaven, but the surge and thunder waxes, wanes, wastes itself; the soul has stormed itself to slumber. The molto piu lento of this scherzo is, by consent, one of Chopin's masterpieces. It is written in the richly colored, luscious key of B major. It is so fragrant, so replete with woven enchantment, that the air becomes divinely dense. With broken tenths, Chopin produces subtle effects It is all a miracle of tender beauty, and is like some old world Armida's garden, when time was young and men and women lived to love and not to sorrow. It is only comparable to the B major episode in the B minor étude or to the Tuberose nocturne of the same key. Mark how the composer returns to his first savage mood! It is a picture of contrasted violence. But beware of the da capo. It grows wearisome. Far better repeat the first section only and attack the coda — the finest coda ever made by the master. I know nothing of his that can equal its boldness, its electrifying ride across country, its almost barbaric impetuosity. The heavy accentuation on the first note of every bar must not blind one's rhythmical sense to the second beat in the left hand, which is likewise accented. This produces a mixed rhythm that greatly adds to the general murkiness and despair of the finale. Those daring chordal dissonances, so logical, so effective, how they must have agitated and scratched the nerves of Chopin's contemporaries! And they must be vigorously insisted upon; no veiled half lights, for the worst is over; the ships are burned; nothing remains but the awful catastrophe. To his death goes this musical Childe Roland, and the dark tower crumbles and creation crumbles at the close. The scherzo ends in chaos, overwhelming, supreme!

I think it was Tausig who first taught his pupils to use the interlocked octaves at the close instead of the chromatic scale in unison. I suppose Liszt did it before anyone else; he always thought of such things, even if the composer did not. I doubt not but that Chopin would have objected to the innovation, although it seems admissible. After the furious Hercules-vein of the coda, to finish with a chromatic scale sounds tame and ineffectual.

Even though the sneer, the peevishness and fretfulness of a restless, unhappy, sick-brained man disturb it, the C sharp minor scherzo is yet the most dramatic, the most finely moulded of the six. It is capricious to madness, but the dramatic quality is unmistakable. It seethes with scorn, if such an extravagant figure is permissible. It is all extravagance, fire and fury, but it signifies something. Just a word about the tempo. Nearly all the scherzi are marked presto, but it should be remembered that it is the presto of Chopin's day, and, above all, of Chopin's piano action. The action of the pianos of his time, especially of the Pleyel piano, was superlatively light and elastic. The Chopin tempi should be moderated, as Theodore Kullak has so often insisted. You lose in ponderability and dignity by adopting the swift, old-fashioned time markings. The first part of the B minor scherzo may be taken at a presto — a comfortable presto, the scherzo in E must be played presto; also the one in E flat; but where the thought takes on a graver hue, where majesty of utterance or nobility of phrase are to be considered, moderate your pulses, I conjure you, master pianists. The C sharp minor scherzo is an especial sufferer from a too hurried speed. The architectonics are consequently blurred, details jumbled and the indescribable power of the piece lost. And if you start out with such a fiery presto, where will you get your contrast of speed in the coda, which should be fairly shot out from your finger-tips? Or would you emulate Schumann and start in with a prestissimo possible and follow with still more of a prestissimo? You remember his sonata? Try a presto by all means, but remember the heavier tone mass of the modern piano. This scherzo is a massive composition, yet full of fitful starts and surprises. The bits of chorale in the trio are hugely Chopin as to fioritura and harmonic basis. More than all the others this one reminds you of some pulse-stirring drama. It is audacious and declamatory. Even in the meno mosso it never tarries, and the coda is built of one of those familiar figures cumulative in effect through repetition and all written eminently for the instrument. The scherzo in C sharp minor is grotesque; it is original. It has affinities with the darkling conceptions of Poe, Coleridge, Hoffman, and is Heine-like in its bitter irony. It is like some fantastic, sombre pile of disordered farouche architecture, and about it hovers perpetual night and the unspeakable and despairing things that live in the night. It is a tale from Poe's "iron bound, melancholy volume of the magi," and on its face is written the word Spleen. Chopin might have said with Poe: "Then I grew angry and cursed, with the curse of Spleen, the river and the lilies and the wind and the forest and the heavens and the thunder and the sighs of the water lilies. And they became accursed and were still. And the moon ceased to totter up its pathway to heaven—and the thunder died away—and the lightning did not flash—and the clouds hung motionless—and the waters sunk to their level and remained—and the trees ceased to rock—and the water lilies sighed no more—and the murmur was heard no longer from among them, nor any shadow of sound throughout the vast illimitable desert. And

I looked upon the characters of the rock, and they were changed, and the characters were Spleen."

All this was told in the dreary region in Lybia by the borders of the Zaïre, where the waters have a sickly and saffron hue. But Poe wrote the word Silence, which I have changed to Spleen. Three of the Chopin scherzi are the very outpourings of a soul charged with the spiritual spleen of this age of disillusionment.

III

Mr. Krehbiel once wrote, in discussing the question of the re-scoring of the Chopin concertos: "It is more than anything else a question of taste that is involved in this matter and, as so often happens, individual likings, rather than artistic principles, will carry the day."

It is admitted at the outset by all musicians that the orchestrations of the two concertos in E and F minor of Chopin are meagre and conventional, not to say hackneyed.

Written in the pre-Beethoven style they simply rob the piano soli of their incomparable beauty, become a clog instead of an aid, and have done more to prejudice musicians against Chopin than any other compositions he has written. That they were penned by Chopin himself is more than doubtful, as his knowledge of instrumentation was somewhat slender, and the amazing fact will always remain that while his piano compositions are ever fresh and far removed from all that is trite or commonplace, the orchestration of his concertos is irksome and uninteresting to a degree. In both concertos the opening tuttis are long and take off all the cream and richness of the soli that follow.

The tone of the piano can scarcely vie with that of the orchestra, yet in the first movement of the E minor concerto the lovely, plaintive solo of the first subject in E minor is deliberately played through; the audience and the pianist must patiently wait until it is finished and then, like an absurd anti-climax, the piano breaks in, repeating the same story, only dwarfed and colorless in comparison. In the Tausig version of the E minor opening the tutti differs, in that it omits entirely the piano solo, contenting itself after the first theme, with the small secondary subject in E minor that is afterward played by the piano. Then come the rich opening E minor chords on the piano, and we are once more plunged in medias res without further ado.

The orchestral tutti before the piano enters in C major, is in the Tausig version very effective despite the dreaded trombones. It must be admitted that here we get some Meistersinger color which is — so the story runs — because Wagner had a hand in the arrangement. Certainly Tausig submitted it to him for judgment.

The orchestral canvas is broadened, the tints brighter, deeper, richer and offering a better background for the jewelled passage work of the piano.

The brass choir is so balanced as to float the staccato tone of the piano, giving it depth and sonority.

Take for example the horn pedal-point in E, which occurs in the middle of the romanza where the piano has the delicate, crystalline chromatic cadenza of three bars only. What a stroke of genius for Tausig to introduce the brass here! It floats the fairy-like progressions of the solo and in what ethereal hues! But orthodox pianists will say this is not Chopin, and raise their Czerny-hands in horror.

The changes in the piano parts of the first movement of the E minor concerto are effective, they in no sense destroy the integrity of the ideas; where there is a chromatic scale in unison, Tausig breaks it into double sixths and fourths and chordal figures which are not simplifications or mere pyrotechnics but decidedly more "pianistic" and brilliant.

One thing seems to be forgotten in discussing Chopin piano literature — his music is more than abreast of our times. Consider the fantasy, opus 49, the scherzi, the ballades, the sonatas — the two later ones — the études and it will be seen that the figures are modern even to novelty; that Schumann, Liszt and Rubinstein borrowed, even if they amplified, and Tausig, if he did alter a few details, did not commit a sin against good taste. Carl Tausig of all virtuosi penetrated deeper into the meanings of the Polish tone-poet, interpreting his music in an incomparable manner.

As regards the coda of the first movement of the E minor concerto Tausig simply takes the awkward trill from the left hand and gives it to the 'celli and contrabasso and the piano plays the passage in unison. Most pianists, Rosenthal excepted, acknowledge that the trill is both distracting and ineffective.

The chromatic work at the end of this movement is broad and infinitely more klaviermässig than the older version, the piano closing at the same moment with the orchestra, the audience not being compelled to listen to cadences of the Hummel type to the bitter end. The piano part of the second movement is hardly touched by Tausig; it could not be improved, but the orchestration is so spiritualized and so delicately colored that even a purist may not groan in disapproval.

Against the Tausig version of the rondo the war of complaint is frequently raised. "What, he dares to tamper with the very notes, introducing sixteenths where Chopin wrote eighths!" Yes, this is true, but what an improvement! How much brighter and livelier the rhythm sounds; how much more joyful and elastic! and when the piano part enters it is with added zest we listen to its cheerful song. It is a relief too, when the flute and oboe take up the theme, the piano contenting itself with a trill. The other changes in the solo part in this movement are all in admirable taste and effective but they are not easier to play than the original. The movement loses none of its freshness by the additions, while it gains in tone and dignity. The octaves at the end destroy in some degree the euphony but add in brilliancy. It is seldom one hears them played with clearness and lightness; but when pounded out they become distressingly monotonous.

If a concerto is an harmonious relationship between the solo instrument and the orchestra then the Tausig version of the E minor concerto fulfils perfectly the idea. Of course if a poor conductor who wishes to make a scandal out of each tutti takes hold of the work and a mediocre pianist attempts the solo part, critics may indeed carp and say that Tausig has spoiled the concerto with his additions.

The argument that holds good in the case of added accompaniments of Robert Franz to Handel is the same here but best of all remains the unalterable fact that the Tausig version is more effective and what pianist can resist such an argument! Tausig in the E minor and Richard Burmeister in the F minor concerto have given these two works of Chopin a better frame; the picture appears clearer and more beautiful, details becoming more significant making both works better understood.

Mr. Burmeister has not only re-orchestrated the F minor concerto, but his cadenza at the close of the first movement — a cadenza that embodies in an admirable manner the spirit of its themes — in reality supplies a missing coda. There are also some important changes in the last movement. Mr.

Krehbiel justly says, Tausig's emendations have greatly added "to the stature of the concerto."

IV

George Mathias has sketched Chopin in a few sincere, exquisite strokes. His alluring, hesitating, gracious, feminine manner and air of supreme distinction are touched upon, and M. Mathias — dear, charming old gentleman, how well I remember him in 1879! — speaks of Chopin's shoulders, held high after the style of the Poles. Chopin often met Kalkbrenner, his antipodes in everything but breeding. Chopin's coat was buttoned high but the buttons were black; Kalkbrenner's were gold. And how Chopin disliked the pompous old pianist, with his airs and stinginess. As Mathias writes with glee of the idea of Chopin's profiting from the instructions of Kalkbrenner:

"Je crois qu'il n'y a eu qu'une leçon de prise," he adds most emphatically.

At Louis Viardot's Chopin met Thalberg, and that great master of the arpeggio and also of one of the finest singing touches ever heard on a keyboard, received with haughty humility the Polish pianist's compliments, not quite believing in their sincerity. Perhaps he was right, for Chopin made mock of his mechanical style when his back was turned; his imitation of the Moïse fantasy being astoundingly funny, according to Mathias.

"What a jury of pianists," he cries, "in the old days of the Salle Erard! Doehler, Dreyschock, Leopold de Meyer, Zimmerman, Thalberg, Kalkbrenner — how they all curiously examined the Polish black swan, with his original style and extraordinary technique!" A row over Liszt's transcription of Beethoven's Adelaïde is mentioned.

And Chopin, pianist? He played as he composed — in an absolutely unapproachable manner. He would doubtless be shocked to hear his music in the hands of some modern Sandow of the keyboard, torn into unmelodic splinters, yet every splinter exhaling a melodic sound under the furious fingers of the misguided pianist. Mathias examines his rubato and settles the much debated question, although Liszt's happy illustration of the unshaken tree with the shimmering leaves, still holds good. Chopin admired Weber. Their natures were alike aristocratic. Once after Mathias had played the noble, chivalrous sonata in A flat Chopin exclaimed:

"Un ange passait dans le ciel."

Mathias first knew Chopin in 1840 in the rue de la Chaussée d'Antin, 38. The house no longer stands, having been demolished by the cutting of the rue Lafayette. Later he moved to the rue Tronchet, number 5. The house is still there. He occupied the rez-de-chaussée. The first piece Mathias brought him was by Kalkbrenner and called Une Pensée de Bellini. Chopin regarded it without horror, then gave the boy the Moscheles studies and the A minor concerto of Hummel. His pupil, Fontana, gave lessons when the master was sick. One day Chopin was ill but received his visitors lying on a couch. Mathias noticed the Carneval of Schumann. It was the first edition, and Chopin on being asked what he thought of the music answered in icy accents as if the work were painful even to know. He could not speak well of music where want of form shocked his classical instincts, so he said as little as possible. And poor old Robert Schumann down in Leipsic pouring out inky rhapsodies over Chopin!

Mathias tells us that Chopin was a simple man — "Je ne veux pas dire simple esprit" — was no critic, was without literary pretensions and not of the intellectual fibre of Liszt or Berlioz. When the aide-de-camp of King

Louis Philippe asked him why he did not compose an opera he answered in that small, slightly stifled voice of his: "Ah, M. le Comte, let me compose piano music; it's all I know how to do."

Bach, Hummel and Field, Mathias says, were his strongest musical influences. You may well imagine his horror if forced to listen to the Ring. A tender-souled creature yet with the fire of a hero in his veins! More masculine, heroic music — free from Liszt's and Wagner's grandiloquence of accent — than the F sharp minor polonaise, some of the ballades, preludes and études, has yet to be written.

V

In the city of Boston, January 19, 1809, a son was born to David and Elizabeth Poe. On March 1, 1809, in the little village of Zelazowa-Wola, twenty-eight miles from Warsaw, in Poland, a son was born to Nicholas and Justina Chopin. The American is known to the world as Edgar Allan Poe, the poet; the Pole as Frederic François Chopin, the composer. October 7, 1849, Edgar Poe died neglected in Washington Hospital at Baltimore, and October 17, 1849, Frederic Chopin expired in Paris surrounded by loving friends. Poe and Chopin never knew of each other's existence yet — a curious coincidence — two supremely melancholy artists of the beautiful lived and died almost synchronously.

It would be a strained parallel to compare Chopin and Poe at many points yet the chronological events referred to, are not the only comparisons that might be made without the fear or flavor of affectation. There are parallels in the soul-lives as well as in the earth-lives of these two men — Poe and Chopin seem ever youthful — that may be drawn without extravagance. True, the roots of Chopin's culture were more richly nurtured than Poe's, but the latter, like a spiritual air plant, derived his sustenance none know how. Of Poe's forbears we may hardly form any adequate conception; his learning was not profound, despite his copious quotations from almost forgotten and recondite authors; yet his lines to Helen were written in boyhood. The poet in his case was indeed born, not made. Chopin, we know, had careful training from the faithful Elsner; but who could have taught him to write his opus 2, the variations over which Schumann rhapsodized, or even that gem, his E flat nocturne — now, alas! somewhat stale from conservatory usage?

Both these men, full fledged in their gifts, sprang from the Jovian brain and, while they both improved in the technics of their art, their individualities were at the outset as sharply defined as were their limitations. Read Poe's To Helen, and tell me if he made more exquisite music in his later years. You remember it:

> Helen, thy beauty is to me
> Like those Nicéan barks of yore
> That gently, o'er a perfumed sea,
> The weary, way-worn wanderer bore
> To his own native shore.
>
> On desperate seas long wont to roam,
> Thy hyacinth hair, thy classic face,
> Thy naïad airs have brought me home
> To the glory that was Greece,
> And the grandeur that was Rome.

I refrain from giving the third verse; but are not these lines remarkable in beauty of imagination and diction when one considers they were penned by a youngster scarcely out of his teens!

Now glance at Chopin's earlier effusions, his opus 1, a rondo in C minor; his opus 2 already referred to; his opus 3, the C major polonaise for 'cello and piano; his opus 5, the Rondeau à la Mazur in F; his opus 6, the first four mazourkas, perfect of their kind;

opus 7, more mazourkas; opus 8, the G minor trio, the classicism of which you may dispute; nevertheless it contains lovely music. Then follow the nocturnes, the concerto in F minor, the latter begun when Chopin was only twenty, and so on through the list. Both men died at forty — the very prime of life, when the natural forces are acting freest, when the overwrought passions of youth had begun to mellow and yet there were several years before the close, a distinct period of decadence, almost deterioration. I am conscious of the critical claims of those who taste in both Poe's and Chopin's later music the exquisite quality of the over-ripe, the savor of morbidity.

Beautiful as it is, Chopin's polonaise-fantaisie opus 61, with its hectic flush — in its most musical, most melancholy cadences — gives us a premonition of death. Composed three years before he died, it has the taint of the tomb about it and, like the A minor mazourka, said by Klindworth to be Chopin's last composition, the sick brain is heard in the morbid insistence of the theme, of the weary "wherefore?" in every bar. Is not this iteration like Poe's in his last period? Read Ulalume with its haunting, harrowing harmonies:

Then my heart it grew ashen and sober,
As the leaves that were crisped and sere—
As the leaves that were withering and sere.

. . . .

In terror she spoke, letting sink her
Wings until they trailed in the dust—
In agony sobbed, letting sink her
Plumes till they trailed in the dust—
Till they sorrowfully trailed in the dust.

This poem, in which sense swoons into sound, has all the richness of color, the dangerous glow of the man whose brain is perilously near the point of unhingement.

Poe then, like Chopin, did not die too soon. Morbid, neurotic natures, they lived their lives with the intensity that Walter Pater declares is the only true life. "To burn always with this hard, gem-like flame," he writes "to maintain this ecstasy, is success in life. Failure is to form habits."

Certainly Chopin and Poe fulfilled in their short existences these conditions. They burned ever with the flame of genius and that flame devoured their brains as surely as paresis. Their lives, in the ordinary Philistine or Plutus-like sense, were failures; uncompromising failures. They were not citizens after the conjugal manner nor did they accumulate pelf. They certainly failed to form habits and, while the delicacy of the

Pole prevented his indulging in the night-side Bohemianism of the American, he nevertheless contrived to outrage social and ethical canons. Poe, it is said, was a drunkard, though recent researches develop the fact that but one glass of brandy drove him into delirium. Possibly like Baudelaire, his disciple and translator, he indulged in some deadly drug or perhaps congenital derangement, such as masked epilepsy, or some cerebral disorder, colored his daily actions with the semblance of arrant dissipation and recklessness.

There are two Poes known to his various friends. A few knew the one, many the other; some knew both men. A winning, poetic personality, a charming man of the world, electric in speech and with an eye of genius — a creature with a beautiful brain, said many. Alas! the other; a sad-eyed wretch with a fixed sneer, a bitter, uncurbed tongue that lashed alike friend and foe, a sot, a libertine, a gambler — God! what has not Edgar Allan Poe been called! We all know that Griswold distorted the picture, but some later critics have declared that Poe, despite his angelic treatment of his cousin-wife Maria Clemm, was not a man of irreproachable habits.

This much I have heard; at the time Poe lived in Philadelphia, where he edited a magazine for Burton or Graham — I forget which — my father met him several times at the houses of Judge Conrad and John Sartain, the latter the steel engraver. Poe, my father has repeatedly told me, was a slender, nervous man, very reticent, very charming in manner, though, like Chopin, disposed to a certain melancholy hauteur; both men were probably poseurs. But after one glass of wine or spirits Poe became an uncontrollable demon; — his own demon of perversity; and poetry and blasphemy poured from his lips. John Sartain has told of a midnight tramp he took with Poe, in the midst of a howling storm, in Fairmount Park, Philadelphia, to prevent him from attempting his life. This enigmatic man, like Chopin, lived a double life, but his surroundings were different and this particular fact must be accented.

America was not a pleasant place for an artist a half century ago. William Blake the poet-seer wrote: "The ages are all equal but genius is always above its age." Poe was certainly above his age — a trafficking time in the history of the country, when commerce ruled and little heed was given to the beautiful. N. P. Willis, Poe's best friend, counsellor and constant helper, wrote pale proper verse while Poe made a bare living by writing horrific tales wherein his marvellous powers of analysis and description found play and pay. But oh! the pity of it all! The waste of superior talent — of absolute genius. The divine spark that was crushed out, trampled in the mud and made to do duty as a common tallow dip! One is filled with horror at the thought of a kindred poetic nature also being cast in the prosaic atmosphere of this country; for if Chopin had not had success at Prince Valentine Radziwill's soirée in Paris in the year 1831 he would certainly have tried his luck in the New World, and do you not shudder at the idea of Chopin's living in the United States in 1831?

Fancy those two wraiths of genius, Poe and Chopin, in this city of New York! Chopin giving piano lessons to the daughters of wealthy aristocrats of the Battery, Poe encountering him at some conversazione — they had conversaziones then — and propounding to him Heine-like questions: "Are the roses at home still in their flame-hued pride?" "Do the trees still sing as beautifully in the moonlight?"

They would have understood one another at a glance. Poe was not a whit inferior in sensibility to Chopin. Balzac declared that if Chopin drummed on a bare table, his fingers made subtle-sounding music. Poe, like Balzac, would have felt the drummed tears in Chopin's play, while Chopin in turn could not have failed to divine the tremulous vibrations of Poe's exquisitely strung nature. What a meeting it would have been, but again, what inevitable misery for the Polish poet!

A different tale might be told if Poe had gone to Paris and enjoyed some meed of success! How the fine flower of his genius would have bloomed into fragrance if nourished in such congenial soil! We would probably not have had, to such a desperate extent the note of melancholia, so sweetly despairing or despairingly sweet, that we now enjoy in his writings—a note eminently Gothic and Christian. Goethe's "Nur wer die Sehnsucht Kennt" is as true of Poe as of Heine, of Baudelaire, of Chopin, of Schumann, of Shelley, of Leopardi, of Byron, of Keats, of Alfred de Musset, of Senancour, of Amiel — of all that choir of lacerated lives which wreak themselves in expression. One is well reminded here of Baudelaire who wrote of the ferocious absorption in the pursuit of beauty, by her votaries. Poe and Chopin all their lives were tortured by the desire of beauty, by the vision of perfection. Little recked they of that penalty which must be paid by men of genius, and has been paid from Tasso to Swift and from Poe and Baudelaire to Guy de Maupassant.

Frederic Chopin's culture was not necessarily of a finer stamp than Edgar Poe's, nor was his range wider. Both men were narrow in sympathies though intense to the point of poignancy and rich in mood-versatility. Both were born aristocrats; purple raiment became them well and both were sadly deficient in genuine humor — the Attic salt that conserves while mocking itself. Irony both possessed to a superlative degree and both believed in the rhythmical creation of lyrical beauty and in the charm of evanescence. Poe declared, in his dogmatic manner, that a long poem could not exist. He restricted the poetical art in form and length, and furthermore insisted that "Beauty of whatever kind in its supreme development invariably excites a sensitive soul to tears." The note of melancholy was to him the one note worthy the singing. And have we not a parallel in Chopin's music?

He is morbid, there is no gainsaying it and, like Poe, is at his best in smaller art forms. When either artist spreads his pinions for symphonic flights, we are reminded of Matthew Arnold's poetical description of Shelley "beating in the void his luminous wings in vain." Poe and Chopin mastered supremely, as Henry James would say, their intellectual instruments. They are lyrists and their attempts at the epical are usually distinguished failures.

Exquisite artificers in precious cameos, these two men are of a consanguinity because of their devotion to Our Ladies of Sorrow, the Mater Lachrymarum, the Mater Suspiriorum and the Mater Tenebrarum of Thomas De Quincey. If the Mater Malorum — Mother of Evil — presided over their lives, they never in their art became as Baudelaire, a sinister "Israfel of the sweet lute." Whatever their personal shortcomings, the disorders of their lives found no reflex beyond that of melancholy. The notes of revolt, of anger, of despair there are, but of impurity, no trace whatsoever. Poe's women — those ethereal creatures whose slim necks, willowy figures, radiant eyes and velvet footfalls, encircled in an atmosphere of purity — Poe's women, while not being the womanly woman beloved of William Wordsworth, are after all untainted by any morbidities.

Poe ever professed in daily life, whatever he may have practised, the highest reverence for "das ewig Weibliche" and not less so Chopin, who was fastidious and a very stickler for the more minute proprieties of life. Am I far fetched in my simile when I compare the natures of Poe and Chopin! Take the latter's preludes for example, tiny poems, and parallel them to such verse of Poe's as the Haunted Palace, Eulalie, Annabel Lee, Eldorado, The Conquered Worm or that incomparable bit, Israfel:

In Heaven a spirit doth dwell
Whose heart-strings are a lute·
None sing so wildly well
As the Angel Israfel.

Poe's haunting melodies, his music for music's sake, often remind us of Chopin. The euphonious, the well sounding, the wohlklang, was carried almost beyond the pitch of endurance, by both artists. They had however some quality of self-restraint as well as the vices of their virtues; we may no longer mention The Raven or The Bells with equanimity, nor can we endure listening to the E flat nocturne or the D flat valse. In the latter case repetition has dulled the ears for enjoyment; in the former case the obvious artificiality of both poems, despite their many happy conceits, jars on the spiritual ear. The bulk of Chopin's work is about comparable to Poe's. Neither man was a copious producer and both carried the idea of perfection to insanity's border. Both have left scores of imitators but in Poe's case a veritable school has been founded; in Chopin's the imitations have been feeble and sterile.

Following Poe we have unquestionably Algernon Charles Swinburne, who is doubly a reflection of Poe, for he absorbed Poe's alliterative system, and from Charles Baudelaire his mysticism, plus Baudelaire's malificence, to which compound he added the familiar Swinburnian eroticism. Tennyson and Elizabeth Barrett-Browning felt Poe's influence, if but briefly, while in France and Belgium he has produced a brood of followers beginning with the rank crudities of Gaboriau, in his detective stories, modelled after The Murder in the Rue Morgue; the Belgian Maeterlinck, who juggles with Poe's motives of fear and death, Baudelaire, a French Poe with an abnormal flavor of Parisian depravity super-added and latterly that curious group, the decadents, headed by Verlaine, and Stephen Mallarmé. Poe has made his influence felt in England too, notably upon James Thomson, the poet of The City of Dreadful Night and in Ireland, in the sadly sympathetic figure of

James Clarence Mangan. Of Chopin's indirect influence on the musical world I would not care to dilate fearing you would accuse me of exaggeration. Liszt would not have been a composer — at least for the piano, if he had not nested in Chopin's brain. As I said before, I certainly believe that Wagner profited greatly by Chopin's discoveries in chromatic harmonies, discoveries without which modern music would yet be in diatonic swaddling clothes.

On one point Poe and Chopin were as dissimilar as the poles; the point of nationality. Poe wrote in the English tongue but beyond that he was no more American than he was English. His milieu was unsympathetic, and he refused to be assimilated by it. His verse and his prose depict character and situations that belong to no man's land — to that region East of the moon and West of the sun. In his Eldorado he poetically locates the country wherein his soul dramas occur. Thus he sings:

> "Over the mountains
> Of the moon
> Down the valley of the shadow,
> Ride, boldly ride,"
> The shade replied,
> "If you seek for Eldorado."

His creations are mostly bodiless and his verse suggests the most subtile imagery. Shadow of shadows, his prose possesses the same spectral quality. Have you read those two perfect pastels — Silence and Shadow? If not, you know not the genius of Edgar Allan Poe. Chopin is more human than Poe, inasmuch as he is patriotic. His polonaises are, as Schumann said, "cannons buried in flowers." He is Chopin and he is also Poland though Poland is by no means Chopin. In his polonaises, in his mazourkas, the indefinable Polish Zāl lurks, a drowsy perfume. Chopin struck many human chords; some of his melodies belong to that Poe-like region wherein beauty incarnate reigns and is worshipped for itself. This then is the great dissimilarity between the artist in tone and the artist in words. Poe had no country; Chopin had Poland. If Chopin's heart had been exposed "Poland" might have been found blazoned upon it.

But, if Poe lacked political passion he had the passion for the beautiful. Both men resembled one another strangely, in their intensity of expression. Both had the power of expressing the weird, the terrific, and Chopin in his scherzi, thunders from heights that Poe failed to scale. The ethical motif was, curiously enough, absent in both and both despised the "heresy of instruction." Art for art's sake, beauty for beauty's sake alone, was their shibboleth.

Will the music of Chopin ever age? Louis Ehlert thinks that music ages rapidly like the beauty of Southern women, and Baudelaire says, "Nothing here below is certain, no building on strong hearts, both love and beauty go." An English critic, Mr. Vernon Blackburn, puts the case plainly: "I do not merely and baldly mean," he writes, "that an artistic production, like man, like the flowers, like the sun, grows older as the years go; I mean that those years do actually steal from it an absolute quality which it once possessed."

Much of the early Chopin has become faded, but the greater Chopin, like Bach and Beethoven, will last as long as the voice of the piano is heard throughout the land.

Frederic Chopin is as Robert Schumann declared, "the proudest poetic spirit of his time."

VI

Fryderyk Szopen — thus Szulc and Karasowski write the name of Poland's great composer — has had varying fortunes with his biographers. He has been much written about, and aged persons who never saw him have published glib memoirs of him. He has been misunderstood and beslavered with uncritical praise, and his friends and pupils have in most cases proved to be his excellent enemies. Chopin to-day enjoys an unhealthy vogue and the fame of him is apt to prove his undoing. A fellow of formidable passions, of dramatic vigor, a man of heroic brain, the woman in his nature and the idolatry of women wove a feminine aureole about his distinguished head, and so he bids fair to go down to posterity the very portrait of a hysterical, jaded, morbid invalid.

But Chopin was all this and something more.

Where is the true Chopin to be found? If you have a pretty fancy for musical psychologizing you will answer that in his music may be discovered the true Chopin, and in no book, pamphlet or pedantic exegesis.

If you believe in biographies there is Niecks' — Niecks who combed creation clean for petty facts and large instances; his two bulky volumes are at once the delight and despair of all Chopinists.

One summer I gave myself over to Chopin and his weaving musical magic. I secured various editions. I read Scholtz and the several editors of the Breitkopf & Hartel edition and enjoyed Theodor Kullak's remarks appended to his edition. In Mikuli I found a moiety to praise and wonder at — there the rubato flourishes like the green bay tree — and indorsed the sympathetic and sane editing of Karl Klindworth, which comes nearer to being a definitive edition than any of them. Von Bülow's version of the studies is partly amusing and partly impertinent — while I carefully avoided all French editions. The French understand Chopin to a limited degree, and they worship in him the qualities that were almost fatal to his genius.

I never heard a French pianist give an adequate interpretation to Chopin's masterworks. If the Germans treat him in a dull, clumsy and brutal manner, the Frenchman irritates you by his flippancy, his nimble, colorless fingers and the utter absence of poetic divination. Without Slavic blood in your veins you may not hope to play Chopin, and all Polish pianists do not understand him.

Here is a list of the books on the subject of Chopin: Frederick Chopin as a Man and Musician, Frederick Niecks; Chopin and Other

Musical Essays, Henry T. Finck; Frederick Chopin, Franz Liszt; Life and Letters of Frederick Chopin, Moritz Karasowski; The Works of Frederic Chopin and their Proper Interpretation, translated from the Polish of Jean Kleczynski by Alfred Whittingham; Musical Studies, Franz Hueffer; George Sand, Bertha Thomas; Letters from Majorca, Charles Wood; Frederick Chopin, Joseph Bennett; Histoire de ma Vie and Correspondence, George Sand; Frédéric Chopin, La Vie et ses Œuvres, Mme. A. Audley; Les Trois Romans de Frédéric Chopin, Count Wodinski; F. Chopin, Essai de Critique Musicale, H. Barbadette; Les Musiciens Polonais, Albert Sowinski; Frederick François Chopin, by Charles Willeby, and whilst rummaging through Scribner's large musical library I found a tiny book called Chopin, which proved to be extracts from George Sand's A Winter in Majorca and familiar material. Then there are fugitive articles almost innumerable, and I have read with interest John Van Cleve's account of the talk he had with Werner Steinbrecher, once a resident pianist of Cincinnati, and a pupil of Chopin. We have all met the man who knew the man who shook the hand of Chopin. He is not always trustworthy, but every stone cast on the Chopin cairn adds to its stature and the legend grows with the years — grows amazingly.

Then there is M. A. Szulc's Fryderyk Szopen, which I have never seen, and if I had, could not read. The fantastic sketches of Elise Polko must not be forgotten, nor the capital study by Louis Ehlert, the latter being most discriminating. Consider, too, the passing references to Chopin in the Liszt, Mendelssohn, Hiller, Heller and Moscheles letters! That loquacious but interesting gossip, De Lenz, has recorded his experiences with Chopin, for he bore to him a letter from Liszt. But use the critical saltcellar in reading De Lenz. His Trois Styles de Beethoven is neither a veracious nor yet a sound book. De Lenz dearly loved a pianist. He was a snob musical in a florid state of culture, and the soul of Thackeray would have hungered to transfix him on the barb of his undying prose. He was a musical tuft-hunter of huge proportions and had spasms over Liszt, Karl Tausig and Henselt. Chopin he handles rather cautiously. The Slavic instinct in Chopin set tinkling in his brain the little bells of suspicion. He sensed at once the object of the Russian's visit; he was almost vitriolic with him and ironical when he played. So De Lenz never forgave Chopin, he etches him with an acid touch, and we are all the richer for it. The unvarying treacle that he pours over the figures of the other three piano artists obliterates completely their outline. The disagreeable prompted the truth.

Unlike Frederick Niecks, I have not had the pleasure of visiting Chopin's pupils, Madame Dubois, née Camille O'Meara; Madame Rubio, née Vera de Kologrivof; Mlle. Gavard; Madame Streicher, née Friederike Müller; Adolph Gutmann, Brinley Richards and Lindsay Sloper. M. Mathias I knew. Niecks met and talked about Chopin with Liszt, Ferdinand Hiller, Franchomme, the 'cellist, a most valuable friend; Charles Valentine Alkan, Stephen Heller, Edouard Wolff, Charles Hallé, G. A. Osborne, T. Kwiatkowski, who painted, according to Niecks, the best portrait of Chopin; Prof. A. Chadzko, Leonard Niedzwiecki, Jenny Lind Goldsmidt, A. J. Hipkins and Dr. and Mrs. Lyschinski. Little wonder then that Professor Niecks has given us two books stuffed with Chopin and two books of the greatest value to Chopin students, because of the material collected and sifted. That Niecks has succeeded in building up, recreating for us a veracious portrait of his hero, I cannot truthfully say. He has refined upon Karasowski, but the latter at least has put the Chopin-loving world forever in his debt. The letters of Chopin were first published by Karasowski, and they are of the utmost importance; genuine human documents. Chopin was not a voluble correspondent. The Liszt story that he would traverse Paris to answer a dinner invitation may be true of his later years, but the young Chopin was gay and wrote gay, chatty letters to his parents and friends. What we lost by the destruction at Warsaw of the Paris correspondence we may never know. That it would divulge much of the George Sand episode is doubtful. Chopin, while not a strict Catholic, was a devout believer, and knowing his mother's piety he naturally tried to conceal the Sand affair. He would have agreed with Mr. George Moore, that when a Roman Catholic abandons his religion the motive is always a woman. Notwithstanding, the Paris-Warsaw letters might have proved a mine of gold. The Chopin correspondence extant has done more to expel the popular phantom born of the vapors in Liszt's brain than anything else. They are neither so witty, so cultivated as Mendelssohn's, nor so profound, rough and pessimistic as Beethoven's, nor yet so gay and naïve as Mozart's letters, they reveal a young man of exaggerated sensibility, of good heart, with a fine sense of humor and of common sense. Culture, in the modern sense, Chopin had not. His was not the intellectual temperament. Music was for him the eternal solvent; the threshing out of musical æsthetics, the tedious argumentations, the polemical side of his art he never relished. He was no propagandist. He disliked controversy and its breeding of bad manners. Chopin was a genius, but a gentleman. The combination is rare. External life was for him a question of good form, and unlike those artists who concern themselves to the degree of madness with questions of form and diction, only to let loose the check reins of morals and manners in real life, Chopin set a high price on outward behavior. He broke with Liszt, as Niecks hints, because he could not endure Liszt's free manner of life. He could forgive Liszt's impertinent emendations to his ballades and mazourkas, but he never forgave a breach of courtesy. This is a big hint for the Chopin hunter.

The something inexplicable to Western imaginations in Chopin's playing and music, which Liszt so elaborately explains with his definition of Zāl, is nothing but the hopeless antinomy of the East and the West. The touch of the Asiatic in Chopin, tempered by French blood and subjected to the attrition of Parisian drawing rooms, will never be quite clear to us. It peeps out in his mazourkas and in the savage splendor of his F sharp minor polonaise. It lurks in the C sharp minor nocturne and runs riot in the last C minor study. It is not the febrile rage of the Gaul nor the Berserker madness of the Teuton and Anglo-Saxon. It is something infinitely more desperate, more despairing. The pessimism of the East is in it, also its languorous and scented voluptuousness. His music, rich, exuberant, exhaling the scent of tuberose and honeysuckle, is too overpowering if transposed to the violin, voice or orchestra. It is so perfectly piano music that its very structure, as well as atmosphere, undergoes a change when taken away from that instrument. True it is that Chopin did not think so profoundly as Beethoven, but there are compensating clauses in his music. Its exquisite adaptability to the medium for which his music was created is no mean achievement, while the merging of matter and manner is so perfect as sometimes to put Beethoven in the shade.

The Chopin rubato is a fetish relentlessly worshipped by many amiable persons who fancy that it is something sweetly and poetically immoral. It is one of the many superstitions that obstinately clings to the name of Chopin. To play Bach's music with more rubato and Chopin's with less would be a boon.

Walter Pater has pronounced in his essay, The School of Giorgione, that music is the archetype of all the arts, the final court of appeal, that "it is the art of music which most completely realizes this artistic ideal, this perfect identification of form and matter." Judged by this Chopin's music—some of his music—is perfect. He says wonderful things in a wonderful way, and in his master eloquence his voice pierces the mist that hangs so heavily about the base of the Bach and Beethoven peaks. It is not always a sonorous voice, but it is singularly fine, sweet and penetrating. Chopin is a dreamer of dreams and not a bard, but when the sword leaps from the scabbard—O, the charm of its design! The ring of steel is the warrior's, the voice is the voice of a man mad with patriotic passion, the shy, feminine soul is completely withdrawn. What a Chopin is this! Think of the A flat polonaise, the ones in C minor, in F sharp minor, and the fantaisie-polonaise, with its triumphant climacteric tutti! Where have fled the tender, confiding, morbid voices of the twilight, the opium-haunted twilight? A man panoplied in shining metallic armor, with closed casque, charges the enemy and routs it, while the song of triumph mounts deliriously to his brains. No! no! Chopin is not for the musical Young Person. He can be very terrible and mordant and he is not often tonic and cheering.

"It is the mistake of much popular criticism," writes Pater, "to regard poetry, music and painting — all the various products of art — as but translations into different languages of one and the same fixed quantity of imaginative thought supplemented by certain technical qualities of color in painting, of sound in music, of rhythmical words in poetry. In this way the sensuous element in art, and with it almost everything in art that is essentially artistic, is made a matter of indifference; and a clear apprehension of the opposite principle — that the sensuous material of each art brings with it a special phase of beauty, untranslatable into the forms of any other, an order of impressions distinct in kind — is the beginning of all true æsthetic criticism."

This especially applies to Chopin. His music may not — despite its canonic classicism — conform to the standards of the art of Bach and Beethoven, but apart from its message its very externals are marvellous. Delicate in linear perspective, logical in architectonic, its color is its chief charm. Too much has been written of the Polish element in this music. Chopin is great despite his nationality. His is not map music, like Grieg's. It is Polish and something more. He was first a musician and then a Pole. I suspect that too much patriotism is read into his music by impressionable writers. The Thaddeus of Warsaw pose is dead in literature, but it has survived in all its native pulchritude in the biographies of Chopin. Liszt is to blame for this in his sweet-caramel book about Chopin, a true Liszt rhapsody, which George Sand pronounced "un peu exubérante." Let us once and for all rid ourselves of the dawdling poseur of Liszt, and on the other side avoid the neat, prim, rare-roast beef portrait drawn by Joseph Bennett. Karasowski, in a frantic endeavor to escape Liszt's Camille of the keyboard, with his violets, his tears and tuberculosis, created a bull-necked athlete, who almost played Polish cricket and had aspirations toward the prize ring.

Chopin's heroism was emotional, not muscular.

Jean Kleczynski's book is pedagogic and throws little light on the tradition of Chopin's execution. The true Chopin tradition is lost. If he returned to-day and played in public we would not accept him. However, he builded better than he knew. His works are for stronger fingers than his.

Mr. Finck is an ardent worshipper at the shrine, and in the Willeby book, the latest of the Chopin lives, there is nothing new and there is much that is misleading, especially the arbitrary and half-baked judgments. The last étude of opus 25 is pronounced weak! It really is a masterpiece among masterpieces. Other critical blunders are not worth haggling over. The greater Chopin, the new Chopin that we Chopin idolaters believe will endure, is not the Chopin of the valses, of the nocturnes — interesting as they are — nor of the tricksy, impish mazourkas. We swear by the F minor fantasy, the barcarolle, the F sharp minor, the fantaisie-polonaises, including the one in E flat minor. We think that no more inspired pages have been written than the D minor, the F minor and the B flat minor preludes, and are speechless before the F minor ballade and the E flat minor scherzo — the one in the B flat minor sonata, and the C sharp minor scherzo. These, only to mention a few, are the quintessence of Chopinism; the rest are popular, banal and of historical interest only.

The real Chopin life has yet to be written, a life that shall embrace his moral and physical natures, that will not shirk his marked abnormalities of vision, of conduct, and will not bow down before that agreeable fetish of sawdust and molasses called "Frédéric Chopin," created by silly sentimentalists and rose-leaf poets. Chopin, with all his imperfections full blown; Chopin, with his consummate genius for giving pain as well as taking pains; Chopin, the wonder-worker, is a fruitful and unexploited subject for the devout biographer.

V

A LISZT ÉTUDE

I

WHEN Franz Liszt over fifty years ago made some suggestions to the Erard piano manufacturers on the score of increased sonority in their instruments, he sounded the tocsin of realism. It had all been foreshadowed in Clementi's Gradus, and its intellectual resultant — the Beethoven sonata, but the material side had not been realized. Chopin, who sang the swan-song of idealism in surpassingly sweet tones, was by nature unfitted to wrestle with the tone-problem.

The arpeggio principle had its attractions for the gifted Pole who used it in the most novel combinations and dared the impossible in extended harmonies. But the rich glow of idealism was over it all — a glow not then sicklied by the impertinences and affectations of the Herz-Parisian school; despite the morbidities and occasional dandyisms of Chopin's style he was, in the main, manly and unaffected. Thalberg, who pushed to its limits scale playing and made an embroidered variant the end and not the means of piano playing — Thalberg, aristocratic and refined, lacked dramatic blood. With him the well-sounding took precedence of the eternal verities of expression. Touch, tone, technique, was his trinity of gods.

Thalberg was not the path-breaker; this was left for that dazzling Hungarian who flashed his scimitar at Leipsic's doors and drove back cackling to their nests the whole brood of old-women professors — a respectable crowd that swore by the letter of the law and sniffed at the spirit. Poverty, obedience and chastity were the three obligatory vows insisted upon by the pedants of Leipsic. To attain this triune perfection one had to become poor in imagination, obedient to dull, musty precedent, and chaste of finger. What wonder, when the dashing young fellow from Raiding shouted his uncouth challenge to ears plugged by the cotton of prejudice, a wail went forth and the beginning of the end seemed at hand. Thalberg went under; Chopin never competed but stood a slightly astonished spectator at the edge of the fray. He saw his own gossamer music turned into a weapon of offence, his polonaises were so many cleaving battle-axes and he had perforce to confess that all this noise, this carnage of tone, unnerved him, disgusted him; Liszt was a warrior; not he.

Schumann both by word and note did all he could for the cause and to-day, thanks to Franz Liszt and his followers — Tausig, Rubinstein, d'Albert, Rosenthal, Joseffy, and Paderewski, we can never retrace our footsteps. Occasionally an idealist like the unique De Pachmann astonishes us by his marvellous play, but he is a solitary survivor of a once powerful school, and not the representative of an existing method. There is no gainsaying that it was a fascinating style and modern giants of the keyboard might often pattern with advantage after the rococo-isms of the idealists, but as a school pure and simple it is of the past. We moderns are eclectic as the Byzantines. We have a craze for selection, for variety, for adaption; hence the pianist of to-day must include many styles in his performance, but the foundation, the keynote of all is realism; a sometimes harsh realism that drives to despair the apostles of the beautiful in music and at times forces one to take lingering, retrospective glances. To all is not given the power to summon spirits from the vasty deep and we have many times viewed the mortifying spectacle of a Liszt pupil staggering about under the mantle of his master, a world too heavy for his attenuated, artistic frame. But the path was blazoned by the great Magyar and we may now explore with impunity the hitherto trackless region.

Modern piano playing differs from the playing of fifty years ago principally in the character of touch attack. As we all know, the hand, forearm and upper arm are now important factors in tone production where formerly the finger-tips were considered the end-all, the be-all of technique. The Viennese instruments certainly influenced Mozart, Cramer and others in their styles, just as Clementi inaugurated the most startling reforms by writing a series of studies and then building a piano to make them possible of performance. With variety of touch — tone-color — the old pearly-passage, rapid, withal graceful school of Vienna, vanished, for it was absorbed in the new technique. Clementi, Beethoven, Schumann and then Liszt forced to the utmost the orchestral development of the piano. Sonority, power, dynamic variety and a new manipulation of the pedals combined with a technique that included Bach part playing and the most sensational pyrotechnical flights over the keyboard; these were some of the characteristics of the new school. In the giddiness produced by freely indulging in this heady new wine from old bottles an artistic intoxication ensued that was for the time fatal to pure scholarly interpretation. The classics were mangled by the young vandals who enlisted under Liszt's victorious standard. "Color, only color, all the rest is but music" was the motto of these bold youths who had never heard of Paul Verlaine. But time has mellowed them, robbed their playing of its clangorous quality and when the last Liszt pupil gives his last recital we may wonder at the charges of exaggerated realism. Tempered realism is now the watchword. The flamboyancy which grew out of Tausig's efforts to let loose the Wagnerian Valkyrie on the keyboard has been toned down into more sober, grateful coloring. The scarlet vest of the romantic school has been outworn; the brutal brilliancies and orchestral effects of the realists are now viewed with mild amusement.

We are beginning to comprehend the possibilities of the instrument and — of ourselves. Wagner on the piano is absurd, just as absurd as Donizetti or Rossini. A Liszt operatic transcription is almost as obsolete as a Thalberg paraphrase. Bold is the man who plays one in public. Realism beyond a certain point in piano playing, is dangerous. We are in a transition period. With Alkan the old virtuoso technique ends. The new was preached in piano music by Johannes Brahms whose music suggests a continuation of Beethoven's last period, with an agreeable amalgam of Schumann and Bach. The gray is in fashion; red is tabooed. The drunken, tattered gypsy who dances with bell and cymbalum accompaniment in the Lisztian rhapsody is just tolerated. He is too strong for our polite nostrils. The Brahms rhapsodies say more; they deal not with externals but with soul states. The glitter is absent, brilliancy is lacking but there is a fulness of emotional life, a depth and eloquence of utterance that makes Liszt's tinsel ridiculous. To this new school, not wholly realistic yet certainly not idealistic in its aims, is piano playing and composing drifting. It may be the decadence — perhaps an artistic Götterdämmerung.

The nuance in piano playing is ruler. The reign of noise is past. In modern music sonority, brilliancy is present, but the nuance is necessary — not alone the nuance of tone but of expression. Infinite shadings are to be found where before were but the forte, the piano and the mezzo forte. Joseffy taught America the nuance just as Rubinstein revealed to us the potency of tone. As Paul Verlaine, the French poet, cried: "Pas la couleur rien que la nuance . . . et tout le reste est littérature."

II

"The remembrance of his playing consoles me for being no longer young."

This sentence, charmingly phrased as it is charming in sentiment, could be uttered by no other than Camille Saint-Saëns. He wrote of Liszt and, as the natural son of the Hungarian composer, musically speaking, he is perhaps better qualified to speak of Liszt than most critics; his adoration is perfectly excusable, for to him Liszt is the protagonist of the school that threw off the fetters of classical form only to hamper itself with the extravagances of the romantic. They all came from Berlioz; Saint-Saëns' violent protest to the contrary; only this much may be urged in the latter's favor: a great movement like the romantic movement in music, painting and literature appeared simultaneously in a half dozen places. It was in the air, and catching. Goethe dismissed the whole movement in his usual Jovian fashion, saying to Eckermann: "They all come from Châteaubriand," and this is a sound criticism for, in the writings of the author of The Genius of Christianity and Atala may be found the germ-plasm of all the artistic disorder; the fierce color, the bizarrerie, the morbid extravagance, the introspective analysis — which in Amiel's case amounted almost to mania. Stendhal was the unwilling St. John of the movement that captivated the powerful imagination of Franz Liszt, as it later caused the orphic utterances of Richard Wagner.

Saint-Saëns sets great store on Liszt's original compositions, and I am sure when all the brilliant, empty operatic paraphrases and Hungarian rhapsodies are forgotten, the true Liszt will shine more brightly. How cheap and tinkling are these piano rhapsodies, and how the old bones do rattle! We smile at the generation that could adore The Battle of Prague, the Herz variations and Kalkbrenner's fantasias but the next generation will laugh at us for tolerating Liszt's rhapsodies when Brahms has written three such wonderful examples. Technically the Liszt arrangements are excellent finger pieces. You may "show off" with them and make much noise and a reputation for virtuosity that would be shattered if a Bach fugue were selected as a test. One Chopin mazourka contains more music than all of Liszt rhapsodies, which are but overdressed pretenders to Magyar blood. Liszt's pompous, affected introductions, spun-out scales and transcendental technical feats are all foreign to the wild, native simplicity of Hungarian folk-music.

I need not speak of Liszt's admirable transcriptions of songs of Schubert, Schumann and Franz, nor of his own original songs nor yet of his three concertos for piano. All these are witnesses to the man's geniality, cleverness and charm. I wish to speak only of the compositions for piano solo composed by Liszt, Ferencz of Raiding, Hungaria. Many I salute with the Eljen of patriotic enthusiasm, and I particularly delight in quizzing the Liszt-rhapsody fanatic as to his knowledge of the études — those wonderful continuations of the Chopin études — of his acquaintance with the Années de Pèlerinage, of the Valse Oubliée, of the Valse Impromptu, of the Sonnets after Petrarch, of the nocturnes, of the F sharp impromptu, of Ab-Irato — that étude of which most pianists never heard — of the Apparitions, of the Legendes, of the Ballades, of the mazourka in A major, of the Elegies, of the Harmonies Poétiques, of the Concerto Patetico à la Burmeister, of many other pieces that contain enough music to float into glory — as Philip Hale would say — a half dozen piano composers at this fag-end of the century.

The eminently pianistic quality of Liszt's original music commends it to every pianist. Joseffy once said that the B minor sonata was one of those compositions that played itself, it lay so beautifully for the hand; and while I have not encountered many self-playing B minor sonatas nor even many pianists who can attack the work in a manner commensurate with its content, I am thoroughly convinced of the wisdom of the great pianist's remark. To me no work of Liszt, with the possible exception of the studies, is as interesting as this same fantaisie which masquerades in H moll as a sonata. Agreeing with Mr. Krehbiel and Mr. Henderson, who declare that they cannot find a trace of a sonata in the organic structure of this composition, and also with those who declare this work to be an amplification of the old obsolete form and that Liszt has simply taken Beethoven's latest sonata period as a starting point and made a plunge for futurity — agreeing absolutely with these warring factions, and thus choking off the contingency of an interesting argument, I repeat that I find the B minor sonata of Liszt most fascinating music.

What a tremendously dramatic work it is! It certainly stirs the blood — it is intense and it is complex. The opening bars are so truly Lisztian.

The gloom, the harmonic haze out of which emerges that bold theme in octaves, the leap from the G to the A sharp — how Liszt has made this and the succeeding intervals his own! Power there is — sardonic power, as in the opening phrase of the E flat concerto which is mocking, cynical, but tremendous. How incisively the composer taps your consciousness in the next theme of the sonata, with its four knocking Ds! What follows is like a drama enacted in the nether-world. Is there really a composer who paints the infernal, the macabre, better than Liszt? Berlioz had the gift, so had Raff, so has Saint-Saëns, but thin, sharp flames hover about the brass, wood and shrieking strings of Liszt's orchestra. The chorale, which is usually the meat of a

Liszt composition, soon appears and proclaims the composer's religious belief in powerful accents, and we are swept away in conviction until after that burst in C, when comes the insincerity of it in the following harmonic sequences. Then it is not real heart-whole belief, and after the faint return of the opening motive, appears the sigh of sentiment, of passion, of abandonment which engenders the notion that when Liszt was not kneeling before a crucifix, he was before a woman. He dearly loves to blend piety and passion in the most mystically-amorous fashion, and in this sonata with the cantando espressivo in D, begins some lovely music, secular in spirit, mayhap intended by its creator for pyx and reredos.

But the rustle of silken attire is in every bar; sensuous imagery, faint perfume of femininity lurks in each trill and cadence. Ah, naughty Abbé, have a care! After all thy chorales and tonsures, thy credos and sackcloth, wilt thou admit the Evil One in the guise of a melody and in whose chromatic intervals lie dimpled cheek and sunny tress; wilt thou allow her to make away with thy resolutions? Vade retro, Sathanas! and it is done; the bold utterance so triumphantly proclaimed at the outset is sounded with chordal pomp and power. The hue and cry of diminished sevenths begins, and so this ruddy, moving picture with its swirl of intoxicating colors goes kaleidoscopically on. Again the devil tempts this musical St. Anthony, this time in octaves and in A major, and he momentarily succumbs, but that good old family chorale is heard again and if its orthodoxy is in spots faulty, it serves its purpose, for the Evil One is routed and early piety breaks forth in an alarming fugue which, like that domestic disease, is short-winded. Another flank movement of the "ewig Weibliche," this time in the seductive key of B major, made mock of by the strong man of music who, in the stretta quasi presto, views his early disorder with grim and contrapuntal glee. He shakes it from him and in the triolen of the bass, frames it as a picture to weep or rage over.

All this leads to a prestissimo finale of startling splendor. Nothing more exciting is there in the literature of the piano. It is brilliantly captivating, and Liszt the conqueror, Liszt the magnificent, is stamped on every octave. What gorgeous swing and how the very bases of the earth tremble at the sledge-hammer blows from this cyclopean fist! Then follow a few bars of that very

Beethoven-like andante, a moving return of the early themes, and silently the first lento descends to the subterranean depths whence it emerged; then a true Liszt chord-sequence and a stillness in B major. The sonata in B minor contains all of Liszt's strength and weakness. It is rhapsodic, it is too long, it is full of nobility, a drastic intellectuality and sonorous brilliancy. To deny it a prominent place in the repertory of piano music, were folly.

It is not my intention to claim your consideration for the rest of Liszt's original compositions. In the Années de Pèlerinage, redolent of Virgilian meadows, with soft summer airs shimmering through every bar, what is more delicious than the étude Au Bord d'une Source? It is exquisitely idyllic. Surely in those years of pilgrimage Liszt garnered much that was good and beautiful and without the taint of the French salon or Continental concert platform.

Away from the glare of gaslight this extraordinary Hungarian patterned after the noblest things of nature. In the atmosphere of salons of the Papal Court and the public, Liszt was hardly so admirable a character.

Oh, I know of certain cries calling to heaven to witness that he was anointed of the

Lord! Pooh! if he had not had to cut and run to sanctuary to escape two women we should never have heard of Liszt the Abbé!

One penalty of genius is its pursuit by glossaries and gibes. Liszt was no exception. Like Maeterlinck and Ibsen, he has had many things read into his music; mysticism not being forgotten. Perhaps the best estimate of him is the purely human one. He was made up of the usual pleasing compound of faults and virtues, as is any distinguished man, not in a book.

The Mephisto Valse from Lenau's Faust, in addition to its biting, broad humor and Satanic suggestiveness, contains one of the most voluptuous episodes outside of a score by Wagner. That halting languorous syncopated, valse-like theme in D flat is marvellously expressive, and the poco allegretto seems to have struck the fancy of Wagner, who did not hesitate to appropriate from his esteemed father-in-law when the notion struck him.

He certainly considered Kundry Liszt-wise before fabricating her motif for Parsifal. In the hands of a capable pianist the Mephisto Valse can be made very effective. The twelve great études should be on the desk of every student of advanced technique.

So should the Waldesrauschen and Gnomenreigen and I cannot sufficiently praise the three beautiful Études de Concert. The ballades and legendes are becoming favorites at recitals. The polonaise in E, when compared to the less familiar one in C minor, seems banal. Liszt's life was a sequence of triumphs, his sympathies were boundless, he appreciated and even appropriated Chopin, he unearthed Schumann's piano music, he materially aided Wagner and discovered Robert Franz; yet he had time for himself and his spiritual nature was never quite submerged. I wish however that he had not manufactured the rhapsodies and the Liszt pupil!

VI

THE ROYAL ROAD TO PARNASSUS

I

MANY years ago a certain young man of o'erweening ambition, with a good piano hand and a scorn for the beaten path, conceived the Gargantuan idea that by playing *all* the études written for the piano he could arrive at perfection by a short cut and thus make up for lost time. He was eighteen years old when he began the experiment and at twenty-two he abandoned his task, a crippled, a sadder, a wiser man.

The young man browsed on études by Bach, Czerny, Loeschorn, Berens, Prudent, Ravina, Marmontel, Planté, Jensen, Von Sternberg, Kullak, Jadassohn, Germer, Reinecke, Riemann, Mason, Löw, Schmidt, Duvernoy, Doering, Hünten, Lebert and Stark, A. E. Müller (caprices), Plaidy, Bruno, Zwintscher, Klengel (canons), Raff, Heller, Bendel, Neupert, Eggeling, Ehrlich, Lavallée, Mendelssohn, Schumann, Rheinberger, Alkan, Fétis,

Ferd, Ries, Isador Seiss, Arthur Foote, Anton Strelezki, Carl Baermann, Petersilyea, Krauss, D'Abelli, Golinelli, Berger, Kalkbrenner, Saint-Saëns, Brahms, Dreyschock, Moscheles, Doehler, Carl Heyman, Hans Seeling, Clementi, Thalberg, Cramer, Chopin, Sgambati, Liszt, Hiller, Brassin, Paradies (toccata), Hasert, Faelten, Vogt, J. C. Kessler, Moszkowski, Henselt, the Scharwenkas, Rubinstein, Joseffy, Dupont, Herz, Köhler, Speidel, Tausig, Schytte-Rosenthal, Von Schlözer, Schuett, Haberbier, Nicodé, Ketten, Pixis, Litolff, Charles Mayer, Balakireff, MacDowell, Leopold De Meyer, Ernst Pauer, Le Couppey, Vogrich, Deppe, Raif, Leschetizky, Nowakowski, Paderewski, Barth, Zichy, Philipp, Rosenthal and lots of names not to be recalled.

And about the same delightful chronological order as the above was observed in the order of study.

What could have been the result of such a titanic struggle with such wildernesses of notes? What could have been the result upon the cerebral powers of the young man after such a Brobdingnagian warfare against muscles and marks?

Alas, there was no result. How could there have been?

And music, what became of music in all this turmoil of technics? Naturally it went begging, and in after years the young man, observing how many young people, ambitious and talented, were pursuing the same false track, determined to think the thing out, and first went about it by asking well-known authorities, and finally formulated the question this way: What études are absolutely necessary for a mastery of the keyboard?

Since the days of Carl Czerny — God bless his old toccata in C! — instruction books, commonly known as methods, began to appear. How many I do not propose to tell you. You all know Moscheles and Fétis, the Kalkbrenner, the Henri Herz, Lebert and Stark and Richardson (founded on Dreyschock). That they have fallen into disuse is only natural. They were for the most part bulky, contained a large amount of useless material, and did not cover the ground; often being reflections of a one-sided virtuosity. Then up sprang an army of études. Countless hosts of notes, marshalled into the most fantastic figures, hurled themselves at varying velocities and rhythms on the piano studying world. Dire were the results. Schools arose and camps within camps.

There were those in the land that developed the left hand at the expense of the right and the other way about. Trill and double-note specialists abounded, and one could study octaves here and ornaments there, stiffness at Stuttgart, flabbiness with Deppe, and yet no man could truthfully swear that his was the rightful, the unique method.

Suddenly in this quagmire of doubt and dumb keyboards arose a still small voice, but the voice of a mighty man. This is what the voice said:

"There is but one god in technic, Bach, and Clementi is his prophet."

Thus spake Carl Tausig, and left behind him an imperishable edition of Clementi!

It was Tausig's opinion that Clementi and Chopin alone have provided studies that perfectly fulfil their intention. It was Tausig's habit to make use of them before all others, in the school for the higher development of piano playing of which he was the head. He also used them himself. Furthermore he asserted that by means of those studies Clementi made known and accessible the entire piano literature from Bach, who requires special study, to Beethoven, just as Chopin and Liszt completed the scale of dazzling virtuosity.

The Gradus was one great barrier — a mighty one, indeed — against the influx of barren, mechanical or nonsensical études for the piano. Just read the incomplete list above, and does not your head wither as a fired scroll at the prospect of studying such a vast array of notes? Then came Von Bülow with his Cramer edition, and another step was taken in the boiling down movement. Moreover the clever Hans took the reins in his hands, and practically said in his preface to the Cramer edition: "Here is *my* list; take and study it. You will then become a pianist — if you have talent." Here is his list:

Lebert and Stark — abomination of angular desolation; Aloys Schmitt exercises, with a touch of Heller to give flavor and flesh to the old dry bones; Cramer (Bülow), St. Heller, op. 46 and 47; Czerny daily exercises, and the school of legato and staccato; Tausig's Clementi; Moscheles, op. 70; Henselt, op. 2 and 5, and as a bridge Haberbier's Études Poésies; Moscheles, op. 95, characteristic studies; Chopin, ops. 10 and 25, glorious music; Liszt studies, Rubinstein studies, and finally, as a "topper," C. V. Alkan with Theodor Kullak's octave studies on the side.

Now this list is not bad, but it is nearly twenty-five years since it was made, and in this quintessentializing age, a quarter of a century means many revolutions in taste and technic. Condense, condense is the cry, and thereupon rose Oscar Raif, who might be called the Richard Wagner of piano pedagogues, for with one wave of his wand he would banish all études, substituting in their stead music, and music only. Pick out the difficulties of a composition for slow practice, said Mr. Raif, and you will save time and wear and tear on the nerves.

Raif made a step in piano pedagogy, nihilistic though it seemed, and to-day we have those remarkable daily studies of Isidor Phillip, which are a practical demonstration of Raif's theory.

Then came forward a few reasoning men who said: "Why not skeletonize the whole system of technic, giving it in pure, powerful but small doses to the student?" With this idea Plaidy, Zwintscher, Mason and Mathews, Germer, Louis Koehler and Riemann have published volumes literally epitomizing the technics of the piano. Dr. William Mason in his Touch and Technic further diversifies this bald material by making the pupil attack it with varying touches, rhythms and velocities.

Albert R. Parsons, in his valuable Synthetic Method, makes miracles of music commonplaces for the tender, plastic mind of childhood. But all these, while training the mind and muscles, do not fringe upon the problem the young man attempted to solve. That problem related to studies only. His hand was supposed to be placed — in a word — to be posed.

He incidentally found that Heinrich Germer's Technics or Mason's Touch and Technic were sufficient to form the fingers, wrist, forearm and upper arm; that on a Virgil clavier every technical problem of the flat keyboard could be satisfactorily worked out, and then arose the question: What studies are absolutely essential to the pianist who wishes to go to the technical boundaries of the flat keyboard?

Technics alone would not do, for you do not get figures that flow nor the sequence of musical ideas, nor musical endurance, not to mention style and phrasing. No one work on technic blends all these requisites. Piano studies cannot be absolutely discarded without a serious loss; one loses the suavity and simplicity of Cramer, a true pendant of Mozart; the indispensable technics and foundational tone and touch of Clementi, a true forerunner of Beethoven, and then what a loss to piano literature would be the destruction of the studies of Chopin, Liszt and Rubinstein!

No; there lurks an element of truth in the claims of all these worthy thinkers, experimenters and seekers after the truth. Our young man, who was somewhat of an experimental psychologist, knew this, and earnestly sought for the keystone of the arch, the arcanum of the system, and after weary years of travail found it in Bach — great, good, glorious, godlike Johann Sebastian Bach, in whose music floats the past, present and future of the tone art. Mighty Bach, who could fashion a tiny prelude for a child's sweet fingers, a Leonardo da Vinci among composers, as Beethoven is their Michel Angelo, Mozart their Raphael.

With the starting point of the first preludes and exercises of Bach the young groper found that he had his feet, or rather his hands, on terra firma, and proceeded with the two and three part inventions and the suites, English and French, and the great forty-eight preludes and fugues in the Well Tempered Clavichord, not forgetting the beautiful A minor fugue with its few bars of prelude.

Before the Clavichord is reached the pupil's hand is ready for Cramer, and some of these beautiful music pieces, many poetical in the extreme, may be given. What could follow Cramer more fitly than Clementi, Tausig's Clementi? A great teacher as well as a great virtuoso, Tausig pinned his faith to these studies, and so does that other great virtuoso. Bach was also Chopin's daily bread.

In Clementi one may discern all the seeds of modern piano music, and studying him gives a nobility of tone, freedom of style and a surety of finger that may be found in no other collection. Tausig compressed Clementi into twenty-nine examples, which may with discrimination be reduced to fifteen for practical use. The same may be said of Bülow's Cramer, not much more than half being really necessary.

Bülow's trinity of Bs — Bach, Beethoven and Brahms — may be paralleled in the literature of piano studies by a trinity of Cs — Cramer, Clementi and Chopin. And that leads to the great question, How is that ugly gap, that break, to be bridged between Clementi and Chopin? Bülow attempts to supply the bridge by a compound of Moscheles, Henselt and Haberbier, which is obviously tedious, and in one case — Henselt — puts the cart before the horse.

I believe the gap can be safely crossed by using the two very valuable Hummel concertos in A and B minor, for between Chopin — the early Chopin — and Hummel there is a certain resemblance. Some of Hummel's passage work, for example, is singularly like Chopin's juvenile style, and Chopin, as everyone knows, was extremely fond of the Hummel concertos. Of course the resemblance is an external one; spiritually there is no kinship between the sleek pianist of Weimar and the genius of Warsaw.

Yet pieces and concertos do not quite serve the purpose, and may the Fates and Joseffy pardon me for the blasphemy, but I fear I do not appreciate the much vaunted Moscheles studies. To be sure, they are fat, healthy, indeed, almost buxom, but they lack just a pinch of that Attic salt which conserves Cramer and Clementi. Understand, I do not mean to speak irreverently of Moscheles. I think that his G minor concerto is the greatest conservatory concerto ever written, and his various Hommages for two dry pianists serve the agreeable purpose of driving a man to politics. I wish merely to estimate the op. 70, 95 and 51 from the viewpoint of a utilitarian.

There is nothing in op. 70 that has not been done far better by contemporaries of the composer. For instance, the double note study is weak when compared with that best of all double note studies, Czerny's toccata in C. En passant, that is one of the most remarkable special studies ever written, and is certainly number one in the famous trio of double-note études, the other two being the Schumann toccata and Chopin's G sharp minor study. Include by all means the Czerny toccata in your list, and get the Moszkowski edition, which is remarkable for nothing except that it omits the celebrated misprint at the close of the original edition.

There are studies by Kalkbrenner noticeable for their virtuoso character. Ries, too, has done some good work, notably the first of the set in the Peters' edition. Then there is Edmund Neupert. His hundred daily exercises are really original, and contain new technical figures, and his études in the Edition Peters are charming. They suggest Grieg, but a more virile, masterful Grieg.

Take the Thalberg studies; how infinitely more "pianistic" and poetic than the respectable Moscheles! I know that it is the fashion of the day to sneer at Thalberg and his machine-made fantaisies, but we should not be blind to the beauties of his Art of Singing on the Piano, his études, op. 26, one of them in C, a tremolo study, being more useful than Gottschalk's famous Tremolo, not forgetting the op. 45, a very pretty theme in repeated notes.

Thalberg has written music that cannot be passed over by any fair-minded teacher or pupil. Another objection to Moscheles is that he is already old-fashioned. His style is rococo, his ornamentation trite and much of his work stale. Study him if you will; a half dozen of his études will suffice; but do not imagine that he prepares the hand for Henselt or Chopin, as Von Bülow so fondly fancied.

There is one man might be suggested — a composer who is as much forgotten as Steibelt, who wrote a Storm for the piano, and thought that he was as good a man as Beethoven. Have you ever heard of Joseph Christoph Kessler?

It is difficult to discover much about him, except that Chopin dedicated the German edition of his preludes, op. 28, "à Monsieur J. C. Kessler." This same Kessler was born in Augsburg in 1800; he studied philosophy as well as music at Vienna, and at Lemberg in the house of his patron, Count Potocki, he composed his op. 20, twenty-four studies, dedicated to J. N. Hummel. Kessler was a brilliant pianist, met Chopin at Warsaw, and later dedicated to him his twenty-four preludes, op. 31. He was highly thought of by Kalkbrenner, and Fétis, and Moscheles incorporated some of his études in their Method of Methods. In 1835 Kessler attracted Schumann's attention, and that great critic said that the pianist had good stuff in him. "Mann von geist und sogar poetischem geist," he wrote, but somehow his music fell into disuse and is hardly ever heard. Fancy a pianist playing a Kessler étude in concert, yet that is what Franz Liszt did, and though the studies themselves hardly warrant a concert hearing, there is much that is brilliant, effective and eminently solid in many of them.

Kessler died at Vienna, January 13, 1872.

Let us examine more closely these studies. In four books, published by Haslinger, they are too bulky, besides being fingered badly. Out of the twenty-four there are ten well worthy of study. The rest are old-fashioned. Book I., No. 1, is in C and is a melody in broken chords that is peculiarly trying to the fourth finger. The stretches are modern and the study is very useful. No. 2, in A minor, is an excellent approach to all interlocking figures occurring in modern piano music. This, too, is very valuable. No. 3 I can recommend, for it is a melody in chord skips. No. 4 is very useful for the development of the left hand. No. 5 is confusing on account of hand crossing, and it could be dispensed with, while No. 6 serves the same purpose as No. 4. If you can play Nos. 4 and 6 of Kessler you need not fear the C minor or C sharp minor studies of Chopin, wherein the left hand plays such an important part.

Book II. has a study — No. 8 — in octaves which might be profitable but I shall not emphasize its importance, for the Kullak octave school should never be absent from your piano rack. No. 10, however — a unisono study — is very good and is a foundation study for effects of this sort. It might be practised before attacking the last movement of the B flat minor sonata of Chopin.

But that about comprises all of value in the volume. Book III. has little to commend — a study, No. 13, same stiff, nasty figures for alternate hands; No. 15, for the wrist, excellent as preparation for Rubinstein's staccato étude, and No. 18, some Chopin-like figuration for the right hand. Book IV. contains but three studies: No. 20 for left-hand culture. No. 21 for stretches and a facile thumb, and No. 24, a very stiff study, which is bound to strengthen the weaker fingers of the hand. Look at these Kessler studies, or, better still, study a dozen of them, and you will find the bridge between Clementi and Chopin, and a very satisfactory bridge at that; for to the solidity of Clementi, Kessler has added a modern technical spirit. One year's experience with Kessler would make you drop your goody-goody Moscheles, or at least play him for the historical interest only.

Naturally every pupil cannot be mentally pinioned to the same round of studies. There are many charming studies before Cramer; for instance Heller; try Eggeling and Riemann as preparatory to Bach, Jadassohn's scholarly preludes and fugues with a canon on every page, and in the C sharp minor prelude and fugue you will find much good, honest music.

Then there are lots of pretty special studies. William Mason's Étude Romanza is a scale study wherein music and muscle are happily blended; Schuett's graceful Étude Mignonne, Raff's La Fileuse, Haberbier's poetical studies, especially the one in D; Isador Seiss' very musical preludes, in which the left hand plays an important part; Ludwig Berger's interesting studies, and a delightful étude of Constantin Voñ Sternberg in F, which I heartily commend. Ravina, Jensen and many, many others have written études for which a light wrist, facile fingers and agreeable style are a necessity, but could all be easily dispensed with. We must not forget a little volume called Rhythmical Problems, by Heinrich Germer, of great value to teacher and pupil alike, for therein may be found a solution of many criss-cross rhythmic difficulties. Adolph Carpé's work on Phrasing and Accentuation in Piano Playing, attacks the rhythmical problem in the boldest and most practical fashion.

Works of special character, like Kullak's Art of Touch and Ehrlich's Touch and Technic, should be read by the enterprising amateur.

We have now reached the boundaries of the Chopin studies, that delightful region where the technic-worn student discerns from afar the glorious colors, the strangely plumaged birds, the exquisite sparkle of falling waters, the odors so grateful to nostrils forced to inhale Czerny, Clementi and Cramer. O, what an inviting vista! Yet it is not all a paradise of roses; flinty is the road over which the musical pilgrim toils, and while his eye eagerly covets joyous sights, his feet and fingers often bleed. But how easily that pain is endured, for is not the Mount of Parnassus in sight, and does not every turn of the road disclose fresh beauties?

II

Some have expostulated regarding the admission of Henselt into the Pantheon of pianists — as if we were self-constituted keepers of its key — and the assertion was made that Henselt's day was past, his études — of course with one exception, the Bird Study, — useless for technical purposes, and his music, generally rococo. There is a certain amount of unpalatable truth in all this that jars on one, but nevertheless I refuse to give up my belief in the Henselt études or even in the somewhat artificial and overladen F minor concerto.

This is an eminently realistic period in piano literature. The brutal directness of the epoch is mirrored in contemporary music, and with the introduction of national color the art is losing much of its old, well-bred grace, elegance and aristocratic repose. Norwegian, Russian, Bohemian, Finnish, Danish peasant themes have all the vitality of peasants and all their clumsiness, too. When I listen to this sort of music I see two stout apple-cheeked Bauern facing each other and jigging furiously, after the manner of tillers of the soil. Such company seems odd and out of place when introduced into the drawing room. But with the Henselt, how different! how much at home in palaces he is! His refined, polished speech is never conventional, nor does he tear passion to tatters, after the approved modern manner. A high-bred man of the world, raffiné a bit, blasé, but true to the core — a poet and a musician. No, Henselt must not go, for who may replace him? His gentle, elegiac nature, his chivalry, his devotion to the loved one are distinctively individual. His nights are moonlit, his nightingales sing, but not in the morbid, sultry fashion of Chopin; even his despair in the Verlorne Heimath is subdued. It is the despair of a man who eats truffles and drinks Chateau Yquem while his heart is breaking. But there is a note of genuineness that is lacking, say, in Mendelssohn, who played Ariel behind many musical masks. Henselt is never the hypocrite; he is franker than the Hebraic Felix, whose scherzino nature peeps forth in solemn oratorio, mocking its owner's efforts at conventional worship. Henselt is a dreamer with one eye open; he never quite forsakes the real for the ideal.

But what charming études are in op. 2 and op. 5! What a wealth of technical figures, what an imperative legato is demanded! and then, above all else, touch, euphony! To play Henselt with a hard, dry touch would be Hamlet with the melancholy Dane not in it. I remember reading in the preface to a book by Ehrlich (some études of his) that in the modern sense a beautiful touch was a drawback, for while it might be ever grateful to the ear, yet if it were not colored and modified to suit the exigencies of modern music it would simply be a hindrance. The writer quoted Thalberg as an example of a pianist with a beautiful touch, but invariably the same style of a singing touch. Liszt was instanced as a man whose singing touch lacked the fat, juicy cantabile quality, but whose tonal gamut was all comprehensive, and who could be tender, dramatic, poetic and classic at will; of course this is the modern ideal of piano playing — although the color business is a bit overdone, variety in tinting at the expense of good, solid brush work — yet we cannot dream of Henselt being played with a bad touch. Fancy mangling that delicious Bird Study by a "modern" dramatic touch! Fancy stroking rudely the plumage of this beautiful bird, and have it pant its little life away in your brutal grasp! I have heard pianists play this étude as if the bird were a roc, and they were throttling it Sindbad fashion for its fabulous egg. Ah, Vladimir Pachmann, how that little bird did sing under your coaxing touch! and how tenderly you put it away into its silvery cage when it had trilled its sweet pipe! You triple locked the cage, too, black bearded Pashaw that you were, by playing three chords in F sharp, mounting an octave at a time!

The Henselt studies should not precede those of Chopin; in fact, some of the Chopin studies could be sandwiched in with Clementi, Moscheles, if you study him, and Kessler. Chopin used the Moscheles prelude. But don't fail to study Henselt. He will give you freedom, a capacity for stretching, a sweetness of style that no other writer possesses. Don't believe that all the horde of peasants, clumsily footing their tunes, have come to stay. Form will prevail in the end, and Buffon said, the style is the man. Much later piano literature is rank, vulgar, uncultivated, and is altogether inferior to compositions of the grand classic school. It is all right to put the cart before the horse when you are backing, but there is no progress in the whole school of composerlings who trade only in the volks tunes of their native land. Grieg has been called the Northern Chopin. What a far fetched simile! The Grieg piano music was once delightfully fresh, and it still has a quaint ring, but what a small, restricted genre! He said all he had to say in his sonatas op. 7 and 8, for piano and piano and violin. To attempt to pad his Scotch-Scandinavian shoulders so as to fit the cloak of the great Pole is a silly sartorial scheme.

And a superb maker of style is Chopin! Grieg lacks style, lacks distinction — that is, a fine style — and while I love his concerto with its mosaic of melodies, yet I tire of the eternal yodel, the Scandinavian triolen that bobs up like a trade mark. His ballade in G minor shows more technical invention than the concerto.

What may one not say about the Chopin studies and preludes, the vade mecum of all good pianists who after they die go to heaven to study with Frederic, Bach fugues and his études! Burn every note of all other piano literature and a mine of wealth would still remain.

If you have a bad left hand with intractable fingers always remember that Bach will individualize those fingers, and that old Carl Czerny has written a set of studies for the development of the left hand (op. 399), which, if taken in moderation just after rising in the morning, will lead to limberness and legato. This is only a suggestive aside, however. Albert Venino has written an excellent Pedal School. Many improvements have been made in pedaling, and Mr. Venino has thoroughly handled his subject. Someone has called the pedal "the breath of the piano," "its soul," which is apposite.

For a light hand play some of Mendelssohn scherzos, but remember that, after all, not velocity but tonal discrimination is to be sought for. Read Kullak's remarks appended to the F major étude of Chopin, op. 10. In the Chopin preludes, op. 28, one may discover many rich technical nuggets. If you long for variety while at this epoch you may dig out Theodore Doehler's fearfully and wonderfully made concert studies and get a glimpse of the technic that delighted our fathers. Interlocked chords, trills, tremendous scale passages and vapid harmonies distinguish this style.

Great difficulties were imposed on the left hand at times, followed by mere accompaniment figures, while the right hand flashed all over the keyboard. This is found in the Gottschalk technic, which is but a combination of the fulminating brilliancies of the French school. Single studies about this time might prove interesting.

Joseffy's crystalline étude, At the Spring, is delightful in color and replete with exquisite touches. To play it pianissimo and prestissimo in a liquid, cool, caressing manner is a triumph of technic.

Ill-fated Carl Heyman has in his Elfenspiel given us a glimpse of his wondrous technic. Vogrich's Staccato Étude is very effective. Ferdinand Hiller's rhythmic studies are excellent, and Carl Baermann's studies are solid, satisfying and sincerely musical. Golinelli, a Milan pianist, has left twelve studies which are practically obsolete, though the octave study is occasionally heard. In the set is one in C sharp minor with a glorious rolling bass, which is very effective.

Speidel has written an octave study, and speaking of rolling basses reminds us of that perennial favorite Die Loreley, by Hans Seeling, a talented young Bohemian pianist who died young (1828–62). His set of twelve studies contain some good things such as the Gnomentanz.

I don't know much about Dreyschock's études, except his Campanella, and somehow or other I don't care to. You remember Heine's remark about the "hellish spectacle" his performances presented?

Quite delightful individualities are the Scharwenkas and Moszkowski. Xaver Scharwenka's preludes and studies are among the best things he has done, the concertos not excepted. The staccato étude is deservedly popular, and the E flat minor prelude and F sharp minor étude are models of their kind. The last named is evidently suggested by a figure in Chopin's E minor concerto, first movement, and is well worked out. Philipp Scharwenka has also done good work. Moszkowski's group of three studies is quite difficult; particularly the one in G flat. This latter smacks of artificiality. Nicode's two studies are well made, and Dupont's toccata in B is a very brilliant and grateful concert piece. Sgambati, the Italian pianist, has written some studies which are interesting for people who like Sgambati. They lack originality. Saint-Saëns' six études are very valuable and incidentally very difficult, the rhythm study in particular.

In all this hurly-burly don't forget your Kullak octave school, and if you really wish to disencumber your mind of all these extra studies I have been talking about, just throw overboard everybody but Bach, Cramer, Clementi, Chopin and Henselt. If you wish velocity coupled with lightness and suppleness of wrist, take up old Scarlatti.

III

After Wagner, Brahms. After Chopin? Bülow once confessed that Brahms cured him of Wagner mania. To alter Browning—"Brahms is our music maker now." Brahms, whose music was at one time as an undecipherable cryptogram! — Brahms now appeals to our finest culture. Without the melancholy tenderness of Chopin he has not altogether escaped the Weltschmerz, but his sadness is masculine, and he seldom if ever gives way to the hysterical complainings of the more feminine Pole. Brahms is a man, a dignified, mentally robust man, who feels deeply, who developed wonderful powers of self-control, and who drives the musical nail deeply when he hits it, as he sometimes does.

Could any styles be more at variance than Brahms' and Chopin's? Moscheles declared much of Chopin's music unplayable, and it is a commonplace of the day to dismiss Brahms' piano music as "unpianistic." Brahms' affinity to Schumann is marked; perhaps when the latter pronounced such favorable judgment of Brahms' op. 1 he only acknowledged blood relationship. Brahms tells us different things, however; but as I intend dealing more with externals I will pass by any question of musical content. To the student of the somewhat florid Liszt, Chopin, Thalberg and Henselt school, the Schumann-Brahms technic must offer few attractions. Possibilities for personal display are rare — display of the glittering passage sort. Extensive scale work is seldom found in either composer, and old-fashioned ornamentation gladdens by its absence. Musically, the gain is immense; "pianistically" there is some loss. No more of those delicate, zephyr-like figures — no more sonorous and billowy arpeggio sweeps over the keyboard!

In a word, the finger virtuoso's occupation is gone, and a mental virtuosity is needed. Heavy chordal work, arabesques that might have been moulded by a Michel Angelo, a cantilena that is polyphonic, not monophonic; ten voices instead of one — all this, is it not eminently modern, and yet Bachian?

Schumann came from Bach, and Schumann is foster father to Brahms; but Bach and Beethoven blood also runs warmly in Johannes' musical veins. Under which king will you serve? for you cannot serve two. Will you embrace the Scarlatti, Emanuel Bach, Mozart, Cramer, Chopin, Liszt school, or will you serve under the standards of Bach, Clementi, Beethoven, Schumann and Brahms? Better let nature decide for you, and decide she does with such marked preferences that often I have attended piano recitals and wept silently because the "piano reciter" fondly believed he was versatile and attempted everything from Alkan to Zarembski. What a waste of vital force, what a waste of time!

I have, and value them as a curiosity, a copy of Liszt's études, op. 1. The edition is rare and the plates have been destroyed. Written when Liszt was fresh from the tutelage of Carl Czerny, they show traces of his schooling. They are not difficult for fingers inured to modern methods. When I first bought them I knew not the Études d'Exécution Transcendentale, and when I encountered the latter I exclaimed at Liszt's cleverness. Never prolific in thematic invention, the great Hungarian has taken his op. 1 and dressed it up in the most bewildering technical fashion. He gave these studies appropriate names, and even to-day they require a tremendous technic to do them justice. The most remarkable of the set — the one in F minor (No. 10) — Liszt left nameless, and like a mighty peak it rears its head skyward, while about it cluster its more graceful fellows, Ricordanza, Feux-Follets, Harmonies du Soir, Chasse Neige, and Paysage. What a superb contribution to piano étude literature is Liszt's! These twelve incomparable studies, the three very effective Études de Concert, the Paganini Studies, the Waldesrauschen, the Gnomenreigen, the Ab-Irato, the graceful Au Lac de Wallenstadt and Au Bord d'une Source, have they not developed tremendously the technical resources of the instrument? And to play them one must have fingers of steel, a brain on fire, a heart bubbling with chivalric grace and force. What a comet-like pianist he was, this Magyar, who swept Europe with fire and sword, who transformed the still, small voice of Chopin into a veritable hurricane! But we can't imagine a Liszt without a Chopin preceding him.

Liszt lost, the piano would lose its most dashing cavalier, and his freedom, fantasy and fire are admirable correctives for the stilted platitudes of the Hummel, Czerny, Mendelssohn school. You can't — as much as you may wish to — ignore Liszt's technic. He got out of the piano an orchestral quality. He advanced by great wing strokes toward perfection, and not to include Liszt were to exclude color, sonority, richness of tinting and powerful dynamic contrasts.

Liszt has had a great following; you can see how much he affected modern technic. Tausig felt his influence, and even Schumann, whose setting, however, of the Paginini études is far removed from Liszt's. But Schumann certainly struck out a very original course when he composed his Études Symphoniques. Here a Liszt style is a bar to faithful interpretation. Music, music, music is wanted, with strong singing fingers and a wrist of iron — malleable iron. The toccata in C is an admirable example of not only Schumann's but also of latter day technic.

As in Brahms' polyphonic fingers, great discrimination of tone in chord passages is required here, and powers of stretching that tax most hands to their utmost.

Brahms has reared upon this Schumann technic a glorious structure, whose foundations — Bach-Schumann — are certainly not builded on sand. You may get a fair notion of the Brahms piano technic by playing the figure he gave Tausig for that great master's Daily Studies, and also in his later fifty-one studies. Look at his wonderful variations — true studies; read the Paganini variations; are they not heaven storming? Brains, brains and Bach. His studies on studies are not too entertaining.

One is the rondo by Weber in his C major sonata, the so-called "mouvement perpétuel." This has Brahms transcribed for the left hand, lifting the bass part into the treble. Anything more dispiriting I cannot imagine. It makes one feel as if the clock struck nineteen in the watches of the night. The étude in sixths on Chopin's beautiful F minor étude in op. 25 is an attempt to dress an exquisite violet with a baggy suit of pepper-and-salt clothes. It is a gauche affair altogether, and I fancy the perpetrator was ashamed of himself, for, unlike Joseffy's astounding transcription of Chopin's G flat étude, Brahms' study upon a study is utterly unklaviermässig.

Constantin von Sternberg tells a story about this F minor étude of Brahms-Chopin. When it first appeared Moszkowski was trying it over in the presence of the Scharwenkas and Von Sternberg. Not content with playing the right hand triplets in double-sixths, as Brahms had done, he transposed them to the left hand, went to work rather hesitatingly, saying, naturally enough: "Why not do it this way?"

It out-Heroded Herod, and Xaver Scharwenka could stand it no longer; when Moszkowski stuck for a moment he strode up to the pianist, seized his nose and chin, opened his mouth, gazed in it, and then said in a slightly irritated voice: "That is the worst of these machines; they *will* get out of order sometimes."

Bendel's étude in double-sixths is a good study, evidently modelled after Chopin's G sharp minor study. Zarembski has written a finger-breaker in B flat minor, and the two Von Schloezer studies are by no means easy studies, but there are technical heights yet to be explored. Charles V. Alkan, the Parisian pianist, has concocted, contrived and manufactured about twenty-seven studies, which almost reach the topmost technical notch, and are, to confess the truth, unmusical. They are the extreme outcome of the Liszt technic and consequently have only historical value. Don't play them, for you can't, which remark is both Celtic and convenient.

Rubinstein's op. 23 — his six études — cannot be lightly passed over. The first in F and the well-known staccato étude in C should be studied. He has also written two studies, both in the key of C, one of which is called Study on False Notes, and sometimes the Handball. They are all very "pianistic." Strelezski's five concert studies are very modern and require a cyclopean grip. Nos. 4 and 5 are the most musical. The same composer's étude, The Wind, is an excellent study in unison. The valse étude is artificial.

You can play Balakireff's Islamey, a fantasy Orientale, if you wish some muscle twisting.

No need of telling you of Tausig's Daily Studies. No pianist should be without them. The Rosenthal-Schytte studies are rich in ideas, and Schytte has written some Vortrag studies that are excellent.

Among modern artistic studies Saint-Saëns', and MacDowell's are the best and most brilliant, and Godowsky has made some striking paraphrases of Chopin studies. A novelty are the Exercises Journalières preceded by a preface from the pen of Camille Saint-Saëns. Tausig thought of such a comprehensive scheme as this, and Kullak, in the third book of his octave school, puts it partially into execution. But it remains for Isidor Philipp to work the formula out to its utmost, and the result is a volume unique in the annals of piano literature and of surpassing value to pianist, teacher and pupil.

This volume, I have no hesitation in saying, is the most significant since the posthumous publication of Tausig's Daily Studies. All pianists have felt the need of such a work, and in his dumb-thumb way Oscar Raif taught his pupils that the manner to master difficulties was to walk chromatically about the passages in question. At a blow Philipp demolishes thousands of technical studies.

Philipp's scheme is this: his collection is only for pianists who have a sound ordinary technic, say a technic which enables one to play the Beethoven sonatas of the first and second period, Clementi, Cramer, and of course Bach.

Philipp begins with extensive exercises, for extended harmonies are the keynote of modern piano music. Then follow studies for independence of the fingers, for the left hand alone, for scales, arpeggios, double notes, trills, octaves and chord playing, rhythmic studies and sundry studies that cannot be classified. These are all original, and are the result of the most independent researches. Conciseness is aimed at. They are reinforced by examples from Alkan to Willmers — the latter being the hero of the trill in the annals of piano playing.

Now, suppose you have each day an hour for technical study. You sit down before your keyboard; play one study for finger extension. Here is one on the first page — a terror, but a salutary one. Then take the example — it is from the F sharp minor prelude of Chopin. If you do not care for that there is the peroration of the E minor concerto of Chopin, the trill on B natural in the left hand. Alkan; Henselt (an example from the first study in op. 5 in C) — you can take your choice.

Now for independence of the fingers. Only two examples are given. If you master them you will have ten perfectly autonomous fingers. One is from a study by Alkan and the other from Saint-Saëns, op. 52. This latter is the famous study in A minor. It is invaluable.

Studies for the left hand: one example from the last movement of the Appassionata, you remember the figure in F minor. Others by Beethoven from concerto and variations. Chopin is represented by studies and extracts from the concertos, and a page is devoted to the G sharp minor section of the Revolutionary study, the Tristan and Isolde episode. Liszt, Georges Mathias, Brahms are all quoted with judgment.

Scales: Copious quotations from Chopin, Hummel, the A minor study of the former has a variant which gives the left hand employment. Liszt, Henselt, Rubinstein, the odd little chromatic episode in the last movement of the D minor concerto, and a finger-breaker by Henri Fissot, in which the thumb is treated to convict labor, as it deserves.

We have now reached the arpeggio section. After a lot of figures from which you may select your pattern for the day — notably the arpeggio of the dominant seventh, the most difficult and therefore the most valuable — you may indulge in examples from Beethoven, Chopin, Thalberg — the master of arpeggios — Delaborde, Rubinstein and Saint-Saëns.

Do not forget that these examples are selected from representative works, works that are played and are selected with rare skill and appreciation.

The double note chapter is admirable, although I notice M. Philipp clings to the Chopin fingering in chromatic double notes, the minor third, etcetera. The examples are from Beethoven, Hummel, Weber, Cramer,

Chopin (the first chromatic scale in op. 25, No. 6); Schumann, Litolff, Saint-Saëns, Liszt, Rubinstein, Delaborde, Alphonse Duvernoy, a valuable and ingenious study; Marmontel, and last, but by no means least, Philipp himself. One example of his is from a Bach fugue in D in double sixths!

The trill department — this sounds like the Bon Marché — contains examples from Beethoven, Chopin, Willmers, Doehler, Liszt, Brahms, a monstrous octave trill from the F sharp minor sonata, Duvernoy, Czerny and Liszt. It is as complete as possible.

The octave section contains more modern examples than Kullak. Saint-Saëns, Diémer, Rimski-Korsakoff and Tschaïkowsky are some of the moderns quoted.

Then follow rhythmical examples, skips, tremolo, a good example is from Thalberg's beautiful and sadly neglected theme and variations in A minor, op. 45 and a lot of tangled tricks from the works of Lalo, D'Indy, Bernard, Pierné and other modern Frenchmen. I wish M. Philipp had quoted Thalberg's famous tremolo study in C. It is the best of its class. But to be hypercritical before this ingenious catalogue would be impertinence, even ingratitude. From the maddening mass of classical and latter-day piano literature the editor has selected and fingered a most representative series of the difficulties of piano music. A few bars, at most a page, are given, and we do not wonder that Saint-Saëns called the work a vade mecum for pianists.

Not content with his gigantic task this astonishing Philipp has made another collection of studies for the left hand alone.

His compilation is so complete that I must speak of it in detail. Indeed I could write much on this topic. I know so many students, so many able pianists who have gone through the valley of technical death in search of a path to Parnassus, that I hail these short cuts with joy. Remember I am of a band of admirable lunatics that played all the studies in the world when I was a young fellow! What ignorance, depraved and colossal, was it not?

Czerny, who is old fashioned in most of his studies, has nevertheless written some of the best studies for the left hand solo. He wrote them because no one else would. He looks in his pictures as if he might be that sort of a man.

Philipp the indefatigable has sifted Czerny, and the left hand is treated, not with arpeggiated contempt — most composers write as if this hand was only for accompanying purposes — but as if it were the companion and co-sharer of the throne of digital independence. All sorts — but not too many — of preparatory exercises are there, thanks to the ingenuity of the editor, who must be a teacher of the first magnitude. In addition to Czerny we get passages from Weber, right hand passages transposed, from Mendelssohn, Hummel, Schumann, the first page of the great Toccata in C, transpositions from Bach and Chopin, a big Kessler study, the first study in C of Chopin, the first study in A minor for the left hand — a pet idea of Joseffy's — a transposition from the B flat minor prelude, a capital notion for velocity playing, another transposition of the A minor study in op. 25, hideously difficult. The same with the G sharp minor study, Godowsky has a version for concert performance, but this is for one hand only; the double sixth study in D flat, a Kreutzer violin caprice in octaves in E, a Kreutzer étude in octaves, and the F minor study of Chopin, op. 25, No. 2 in octaves.

The volume ends with a formidable version in octaves for left hand of the last movement of Chopin's B flat minor sonata. This is truly a tour de force.

This clever Parisian has also written six new concert studies. The first is a double note arrangement of the D flat valse. Tausig, Rosenthal and Joseffy have done the same thing. But Philipp has written the trio in three clefs so as to render clear the contrapuntal figure over the melody, which figure is the first theme. His second study is the same valse written for the left hand, the accompaniment being transposed to the right. The third study is the F minor study in triplets of Chopin, most ingeniously transcribed for left hand. Brahms turned this study into forbidding thistles of double sixths. The fourth study is devoted to the G flat étude of Chopin, the one on the black keys. It is in double notes, fourths, sixths and octaves. Joseffy ten years ago anticipated Philipp.

For his fifth concert study I congratulate M. Philipp. He has taken Chopin's first A minor study in op. 10 and turned it into a bombarding chord study, something after the manner of the sombre and powerful B minor octave study. The blind octave is the technical foundation of this transcription. It is very effective. The book closes with a magnificent paraphrase of Weber's perpetual movement from the sonata in C. Brahms and others have transcribed this for the left hand. It is aptly dedicated to the master, a veritable master, Camille Saint-Saëns. I wish I could enlarge on the "pianistic" qualities of this piece. Oddly enough it suggests in a distant fashion Rubinstein's C major study, he one d'Albert plays so masterfully. Phi pp has made the changes in the most musicianly manner.

M. Philipp has credited to Theodore Ritter, now dead, the octave version of the rondo of Chopin's E minor concerto. To Tausig belongs the honor. I wonder why he failed to quote the stunning étude in B flat minor by Franz Bendel? After Chopin's it is the most valuable of all the studies for the playing of double sixths.

Not satisfied with making a unique volume of daily studies, he has out-Tausiged Tausig in the new Études d'Octaves. The studies are after Bach, Clementi, Cramer and Chopin, with original preludes by Dubois, Delaborde, Émile Bernard, Duvernoy, Gabriel Fauré, Matthias, Philipp, Pugno and Widor. I advise you to play Kullak upside down before you touch these new studies on studies—these towering Pelions piled on metacarpal Ossias.

Philipp begins with the E flat study of Clementi, the one in broken octaves; this he transforms to a repeated note exercise.

The first two studies in the Gradus he makes octaves. So far nothing remarkable nor difficult. Then follows the B flat invention of Bach — in two voices — in octaves; the study in E by Cramer treated as a study in sustained tones, like the second section of Chopin's great octave study in B minor. We begin to grow warm over Cramer's first famous study in C, all bedeviled into chords and taken at the interesting metronomic tempo of 116 to the quarter notes. It sounds like a gale from Rubinstein.

As all flesh is grass, so all difficult piano studies become food for the virtuoso. Brahms in a moment of heavy jocundity made night and Chopin hideous with the study in F minor by forcing the sweet, coy, maidenly triplets to immature coquetting with rude and crackling double sixths. Philipp is too polite, too Gallic to attempt such sport, so he gives the étude in unison octaves. It is a good study, but one prefers the original.

Cramer's left hand study in D minor is treated to octaves, and so the A minor study of Chopin in op. 10 is worked up magnificently and is really worth the while to play as well as to practice — a distinction you will observe. But more momentous matter follows. I expected that I should see the day when Weber's so-called Perpetual Motion — the rondo in C — would be played in octaves by children, but I little dreamed of the daring of the latter-day pianist. The tenth study in this book is in interlocked octaves, after the manner of Tausig, and is in the key of B flat minor. Can you guess on what it is built? No less a theme than the last movement of the B flat minor sonata of Chopin, and it is a presto. Tausig is reported to have said that the movement reminded him of the wind sighing over the grave of the beloved, and Joseffy told me that Tausig could play it in octaves.

Like all legends of the sort, you treasure it and grow reverend, but when you see these octaves on the printed page you shudder. Where will technic end? It is worse than Brahms in his stupendous Paganini studies. In a study by Paderewski, The Desert, may be found just such toying with the gigantic, the ineffable. Philipp, with his precise, practical mind, pins his miracles to the paper, and while we curiously study the huge wings of this phenomenal bird we are not attracted. The study is written for a dozen living pianists at the utmost.

Henselt has written some studies which he calls Master Studies for Piano. They are really studies for virtuosi, and should be severely left alone by any but finished pianists. Carlyle Petersilyea once made a sort of technical variante on Chopin's study in sixths in op. 25. Henselt goes upon the principle that pianists grow weary of playing a piece in the same manner; that the fingers become indolent from the fatal facility which follows upon many performances of a composition. So he takes up the familiar difficulty and views it from another rhythmical point of view. He distorts, perverts, alters, and almost roots up from the harmonic and rhythmic soil, the figuration, and believes that with a new aspect, a fresh difficulty, that you will return refreshed in finger and mentally invigorated to the normal version. And the great pianist and pedagogue has accomplished his task with a vengeance.

There are 167 examples; some make you shudder, some cause a smile, all command respect for the agility of the paraphrase, the downright cleverness of the changes. When you have thoroughly mastered the Philipp Daily Studies — which will be never — I commend these Henselt perversions. But may God preserve you from dallying too long in these curious and repulsive pastures, for can you imagine anything more horrible than a pianist assailed in the full glare of a public performance by a Henselt version and unable to resist the temptation!

Some of the perversions are worthy of the consideration of a musical Lombroso. There is the G flat study of Chopin, The Butterfly; Henselt has lots of fun with the piece, and his humor peeps out at the close, for instead of the epigrammatic ending — alas! so seldom adhered to by foolish pianists — he makes an elaborate run and delays the end, a delicate and satiric commentary on the ambitious pounder who will insist on bowling all over the keyboard before he lets go the key.

Chopin is liberally paraphrased, and the version of the E minor valse is fit for concert performance, so brilliant and effective is it. There are examples from Beethoven, Henselt — he has mocked his own Bird Study — Hummel, Mendelssohn, Weber, Cramer, Liszt, Raff, Schumann and Moscheles. Yet one coyly suggests these studies. They are apt to hoist the pianist with his own petard.

I once asked Rosenthal what finger exercises or studies he employed to build up that extraordinary mechanism of his. He startled me by replying "none." Then he explained that he picked out the difficulties of a composition and made new combinations of them. Every rope has its weak spot and in every composition there is the one difficulty that will not down. Master it and you are technically master of all you survey. The whole question may be summed up this way: study a few Cramer, a few Clementi études for elegance and endurance, avoid daily studies except those few that by experience you discover limber up your wrist and fingers. Play the Chopin études, daily, also the preludes, for the rest trust to God and Bach. Bach is the bread of the pianist's life; always play him that your musical days may be long in the land.

VII

A NOTE ON RICHARD WAGNER

I

IF it had been hinted a quarter of a century ago that in Richard Wagner's veins there flowed Semitic blood, roaring laughter would have streaked critical Europe. The race Wagner reviled in speech and pamphlet — although he never disdained its financial generosity — the hated Jew, daring to claim kinship with him, might have set in motion the mighty spleen of the master, and perhaps the world would be the poorer for another Das Judenthum in der Musik. Wagner's hatred of the chosen race is historical. Benefits ever forgotten, he never lost a chance to gibe at Meyerbeer, to flout some wealthy Hebrew banker. Yet gossips have been at work subjecting the Wagnerian pedigree to keen scrutiny. There is a well-defined legend at Bayreuth, at Leipsic, that Wagner was the natural son and not the stepson of Ludwig Geyer, his mother's second husband.

Of course this is not so, for it would make Wagner a half Jew, the actor Geyer being of Jewish descent. Wagner, they say, resembled him more in features, tastes and temperament than he did his putative father, the worthy police magistrate.

A musical authority, whose name I withhold by request, called my attention to the curious fact that the portrait of Wagner's father does not hang upon the walls of Wahnfried. Perhaps as Geyer was the father Wagner best remembered he did him the honor of placing his picture in juxtaposition with his mother's in the Bayreuth home. There is no other sound evidence that may be pressed into service for this fugitive theory. Friedrich Nietzsche, after the rupture with Wagner, openly called him a Jew born in the Judengasse — the ghetto of Leipsic — and this latter assertion happens to be true. Another hot-headed hunter of degeneration, Heinrich Pudor, makes the same statement.

In critical circles there seems to be a disposition to avoid challenging these facts for they asperse the memory of a good mother. Mr. Krehbiel laughs at the story as silly, summoning as witness the fact that Wagner's elder brother resembled him in a striking manner. I place little credence in the rumor, believing it to have originated with Nietzsche and revived later by Pudor. There is much in Richard Wagner's polemical writings — his almost insane hatred of the Jews — and in the sensuous glitter and glow of his music that suggests the imagination of the Oriental. Some of it is certainly unlike any music made by a German — indeed, to me, with their vibratile rhythms, their titanic and dramatic characterization, the Wagner plays suggest the Celt, for the Celt, as Matthew Arnold wrote, has *natural magic* in his poetic speech, and magical in their quality are the utterances of Wagner.

"Was Wagner German at all?" asks Nietzsche, a rabid hater of the Christ idea, who first threw Schopenhauer overboard, only to do the same for his Wagner worship. He continues: "We have some reasons for asking this. It is difficult to discern in him any German trait whatsoever. Being a great learner he has learned to imitate much that is German — that is all. His character itself is in opposition to what has hitherto been regarded as German — not to speak of the German musician! His father was a stage-player named Geyer. A Geyer is almost an Adler — Geyer and Adler are both names of

Jewish families. What has hitherto been put into circulation as the 'Life of Wagner' is fable convenue, if not worse. I confess my distrust of every point which rests solely on the testimony of Wagner himself. He had not pride enough for any truth whatsoever about himself; nobody was less proud; he remained, just like Victor Hugo, true to himself even in biographical matters — he remained a stage-player."

Naturally, all that Nietzsche writes about Wagner may be challenged, although he is fairer to the great music-dramatist than Max Nordau. Nordau really borrowed Nietzsche's denunciatory thunder, and then abused the sadly stricken philosopher for having assailed the musician. Altogether a very Nordau-like proceeding.

I should like to believe, but cannot, that Schopenhauer ruined Wagner. This is one of Nietzsche's favorite contentions. The fact is, the artist was stronger than the philosopher in Wagner. The reflective man in him was generally overcome by the man poetic. Witness Tristan and Isolde, which was composed, as Wagner confessed, in direct defiance of his pet theories. Even the pessimism of the Ring never crowds out the dramatic power of the work. Who would wish to cut from Die Meistersinger Hans Sachs' beautiful monologue? It is the passing of a cloud over the shining sun. All thoughtful humans are pessimistic at times, but the strong man and woman soon tire of the cui bono and find work near at hand. Wagner was caught in the currents of his time, though he really escaped many metaphysical vortices. That he was any more a Christian than a Schopenhauerian at the end of his life I doubt. Wagner was primarily an artist and, as an artist, could not help seeing the artistic possibilities in the superb ceremonial of the Roman Catholic Church; could not help feeling the magnificent story of the Christ; could not escape being touched by the beauties of pity, of redemption, and by the Quietist doctrines of Buddhism filtered through the hard brain of Arthur Schopenhauer. All these elements he blended dexterously in Parsifal, and we know with what result.

Keep in your mind that Wagner the artist was a greater man than Wagner the vegetarian, Wagner the anti-vivisectionist, Wagner the revolutionist, the Jew hater, the foe of Meyerbeer and Mendelssohn, and greater than Wagner the philosopher. It is a mistaken partisanship that attaches to his every word deep significance. He dearly loved paradox, and his versatility was such that he wore many masks. Not that I doubt his sincerity, but the enormously emotional nature of the man, his craving for artistic excitement, his agitated life often led him to write and speak in misleading terms. Wagner was not a Christian; he was not a passive Buddhist — far from it; he was no lover of the Jewry, and his pessimism, like Schopenhauer's, was thin skinned. Both men were desperately in earnest and both enjoyed life — one in execrating it, the other in works of beauty.

II

I have often wondered where Wagner's religion, his art, his metaphysics, in a word his working theory of life, would have led him, had he lived longer. That he had, dimly floating in his extraordinary brain, the outlines of a greater work than Parsifal we learn in his correspondence with Liszt. He died with the Trilogy incomplete, for Tristan and Isolde, Parsifal, and The Penitents, (Die Büsser) were to have been this Trilogy of the Will to Live, Compassion and Renunciation.

Wagner was going to the East with many other Old World thinkers. That negation of the will to live, so despised by his former admirer Nietzsche, had gripped him after he forsook the philosophy of Feuerbach for Schopenhauer in 1854. He eagerly absorbed this Neo-Buddhism and at the time of his death was fully prepared to accept its final word, its bonze-like impassivity of the will, and sought to translate into tone its hopelessly fatalistic spirit, its implacable hatred of life in the flesh.

That the world has lost a gigantic experiment may not be doubted, but that it has lost the best of Wagner I greatly question. In Parsifal his thematic invention is not at its high-water mark, despite his wonderful mastery of technical material, the marvellous moulding of spiritual stuff. Even if Parsifal is almost an abstraction, is not that "howling hermaphrodite," as Hanslick called Kundry, a real flesh and blood creation? It is with no fears of Wagner's power of characterization failing that we should concern ourselves, for the gravity of the possible situation lies in the fact that Wagner had drifted into the philosophical nihilism, the intellectual quietism which is the sweet, consoling pitfall of the thinker who wanders across the border-line of Asiatic religious ideals. The glimmer of Christianity in Parsifal seems like the last expiring atom of Wagner's faith in the value of Christ. That he used the church in the dramatic sense cannot be doubted, and that in the ritual of the Roman Catholic Church he found grateful material, which he employed so deftly yet so reverently in Parsifal, is also incontrovertible; but in Wagner's Christianity I place no faith.

He went to the roots of Christianity, its Buddhistic roots, and there sought philosophical consolation. Nietzsche's attack on Wagner's supposed religious predilections is wide of the mark; no one was less likely to indulge in sacerdotal sentimentalism than Richard of the giant brain.

The speculation is a fascinating one, especially when you remember that he changed the title of his projected work from The Victors (Die Sieger) to The Penitents. First spoken of in 1856, the name was altered a quarter of a century later. Wagner had encountered Oriental philosophy in the interval, and its mysticism had become a vital, integral part of his strenuous intellectual and emotional life.

It is not safe yet to pass judgment on this emotional product of the age; Wagner carried within his breast the precious eucharist of genius. In music he is the true Zeit Geist

III

It was a German critic of acuity who said of the music of Tristan and Isolde, "The thrills relieve each other in squads." Wagner certainly touched the top-notch of his almost boundless imaginings in this supreme apotheosis of lyric ecstasy. A scorching sirocco for the soul are the tremendous blasts of this work. Nothing has ever been written that is comparable with it in intensity, and it is safe to predict that future generations will not hear its double. Wagner declared that when he wrote it he could not have composed it otherwise; it is full blown with his imperfections, his glaring excellences, his noble turgidity, his lack of frugality, his economy of resource, his dazzling prodigality, his riotous tonal debaucheries, his soggy prolixity and his superhuman fascinations.

All that may be urged against Wagner's ways I am, perforce, compelled to acknowledge. He is all that his musical enemies say, and much more; but how wilted are theories when in the full current of this tropical simoon! I have steeled myself repeatedly when about to listen to "Tristan and Isolde" and summoned up all my prejudices, bade my feeble faculties perform their task of analysis, but am breathless and vanquished before the curtain rises.

What boots it, then, to gird critically at an art, a devilish, demoniac art that enchants, thrills and makes mock of all spiritual theories about the divine in music? Here it is no longer on the heights as in Beethoven's realm. The philosophy of Schopenhauer hurled at your head in the pessimistic dualism of the famous love scene availeth not to stem the turbulent, sensuous torrent. Tristan and Isolde is the last word, the very deification of carnalism. Call it what pretty titles you may, wreathe the theme with the garlands of poetic fancy, the stark naked fact stares at you — a strong, brutal, fact. It is the man and the woman, nothing more, nothing less. The love potion does but unloosen their tongues, for both were mute lovers before Brangäne juggled with the fatal brew. Not in the sacred writings of the Jews, not in Shakespeare, are expressed such frenetic passions. The songs of Solomon are mildly Virgilian in comparison. This distinction must be conferred upon Wagner; he is the greatest poet of passion the world has yet encountered. As fiercely erotic as Swinburne, with Swinburne's matchless art, he has a more eloquent, a more potent instrument than words; he has the orchestra that thunders, surges and searches out the very heart of love. A mighty master, but a dangerous guide.

I am not an ardent admirer of all the Wagnerian play-books. There is much that is puerile, much that is formless, and many scenes are too long. It was Louis Ehlert who said that nothing but the sword would suffice, and an heroic sword, to lop off superfluities. To the argument that much lovely music is bound to be sacrificed by such a summary proceeding, let the answer be — sacrifice it. "The play's the thing;" dramatic form must come first, else the whole Wagnerian framework topples groundward.

If you consider, you will discover that Tristan is not the protagonist of this fiery soul drama. He accepts the potion in the first act, gets stabbed in the second, and tears the bandage from his wound in the third. Isolde is the more absorbing figure. It is her enormous passion that breaks the barricades of knightly honor and reserve. She it is who extinguishes the torch that signals Tristan. She summons him with her scarf; she meets him more than half-way; she dares all, loses and gains all.

She is not timid, nor does she believe in prudent measures. Shakespeare in Juliet, Ibsen in Hedda Gabler, never went such lengths. I think that to Wagner must be awarded the honor of discovering the new woman. Isolde's key is high-pitched from the outset. And with what superb wrath she cries:

"Destroy this proud ship, swallow its shattered fragments and all that dwells upon it; the floating breath I will give you, O winds, as a reward"! And Wagner has wedded this dramatic invocation to magnificent music.

The composer often, in the intense absorption of creation, forgot the existence of the Kantean categories of space and time. It requires strong nerves to sit out Tristan and Isolde with unflagging interest; not because it bores, but because it literally drains you of your physical and psychical powers. The world seems drab after this huge draught that Wagner proffers us in an exquisitely carved and chased chalice, but one far too large for average human capacity. He has raised many degrees the pitch of passion, and this work, which I think is his most perfect flowering, sets the key for all future composers.

A NOTE ON RICHARD WAGNER

Let Nordau call us degenerates and our geniuses mattoids, we can endure it. We are the slaves of our age, and we adore Wagner because he moves us, thrills and thralls us. His may not be the most spiritual art, but it is the most completely fascinating.

INDEX

INDEX

INDEX

INDEX

INDEX

INDEX

INDEX

INDEX

INDEX

INDEX

INDEX

INDEX

INDEX

INDEX

INDEX

BOOKS BY JAMES HUNEKER

What some distinguished writers have said of them:

Maurice Maeterlinck wrote, May 15, 1905: "Do you know that 'Iconoclasts' is the only book of high and universal critical worth that we have had for years—to be precise, since Georg Brandes. It is at once strong and fine, supple and firm, indulgent and sure."

And of "Ivory Apes and Peacocks" he said, among other things: "I have marvelled at the vigilance and clarity with which you follow and judge the new literary and artistic movements in all countries. I do not know of criticism more pure and sure than yours." (October, 1915.)

"The Mercure de France translated the other day from Scribner's one of the best studies which have been written on Stendhal for a long time, in which there was no evasion of the question of Stendhal's immorality. The author of that article, James Huneker, is, among foreign critics, the one best acquainted with French literature and the one who judges us with the greatest sympathy and with the most freedom. He has protested with force in numerous American journals against the campaign of defamation against France and he has easily proved that those who participate in it are ignorant and fanatical."—"*Promenades Littéraires*" (*Troisième Série*), *Remy de Gourmont.* (Translated by Burton Rascoe for the Chicago *Tribune.*)

Paul Bourget wrote, Lundi de Paques, 1909, of "Egoists": "I have browsed through the pages of your book and found that you touch in a sympathetic style on diverse problems, artistic and literary. In the case of Stendhal your catholicity of treatment is extremely rare and courageous."

Dr. Georg Brandes, the versatile and profound Danish critic, wrote: "I find your breadth of view and its expression more European than American; but the essential thing is that you are an artist to your very marrow."

UNICORNS

"The essays are short, full of a satisfying—and fascinating—crispness, both memorable and delightful. And they are full of fancy, too, of the gayest humor, the quickest appreciation, the gentlest sympathy, sometimes of an enchanting extravagance."
—*New York Times.*

MELOMANIACS

"It would be difficult to sum up 'Melomaniacs' in a phrase. Never did a book, in my opinion at any rate, exhibit greater contrasts, not, perhaps, of strength and weakness, but of clearness and obscurity."
—HAROLD E. GORST, in *London Saturday Review* (Dec. 8, 1906).

VISIONARIES

"In 'The Spiral Road' and in some of the other stories both fantasy and narrative may be compared with Hawthorne in his most unearthly moods. The younger man has read his Nietzsche and has cast off his heritage of simple morals. Hawthorne's Puritanism finds no echo in these modern souls, all sceptical, wavering, and unblessed. But Hawthorne's splendor of vision and his power of sympathy with a tormented mind do live again in the best of Mr. Huneker's stories."
—*London Academy* (Feb. 3, 1906).

ICONOCLASTS: A Book of Dramatists

"His style is a little jerky, but it is one of those rare styles in which we are led to expect some significance, if not wit, in every sentence."
—G. K. CHESTERTON, in *London Daily News.*

MEZZOTINTS IN MODERN MUSIC

"Mr. Huneker is, in the best sense, a critic; he listens to the music and gives you his impressions as rapidly and in as few words as possible; or he sketches the composers in fine, broad, sweeping strokes with a magnificent disregard for unimportant details. And as Mr. Huneker is, as I have said, a powerful personality, a man of quick brain and an energetic imagination, a man of moods and temperament—a string that vibrates and sings in response to music—we get in these essays of his a distinctly original and very valuable contribution to the world's tiny musical literature."
—J. F. RUNCIMAN, in *London Saturday Review.*

IVORY APES AND PEACOCKS

"Out of the depressing welter of our American writing upon æsthetics, with its incredible thinness and triteness and paltriness, its intellectual sterility, its miraculous dulness, its limitless and appalling vapidity, Mr. James Huneker, and the small and honorable minority of his peers, emerge with a conspicuousness that is both comforting and disgraceful. . . . Susceptibility, clairvoyance, immediacy of response, are his; he is the friend of any talent that is fine and strange and frank enough to incur the dislike of the mighty army of Bourbons, Puritans, and Bœotians. He is innocent of prepossessions. He is infinitely flexible and generous. Yet if, in the twenty years that we have been reading him, he has ever praised a commonplace talent, we have no recollection of it. His critical tact is well-nigh infallible. . . . His position among writers on æsthetics is anomalous and incredible: no merchant traffics in his heart, yet he commands a large, an eager, an affectionate public. Is it because he is both vivid and acute, robust yet fine-fingered, tolerant yet unyielding, astringent yet tender—a mellow pessimist, a kindly cynic? Or is it rather because he is, primarily, a temperament—dynamic, contagious, lovable, inveterately alive—expressing itself through the most transparent of the arts?"
—LAWRENCE GILMAN, in *North American Review* (October, 1915).

NEW COSMOPOLIS

"Mr. James Huneker, critic of music in the first place, is a craftsman of diverse accomplishment who occupies a distinctive and distinguished place among present-day American essayists. He is intensely 'modern,' well read in recent European writers, and not lacking sympathy with the more rebellious spirits. Ancient serenity has laid no chastening hand on his thought and style, but he has achieved at times a fineness of expression that lifts his work above that of the many eager and artistic souls who strive to be the thinkers of New England to-day. He flings off his impressions at fervent heat; he is not ashamed to be enthusiastic; and he cannot escape that large sentimentality which, to less disciplined transatlantic writers, is known nakedly as 'heart interest.' Out of his chaos of reading and observation he has, however, evolved a criticism of life that makes for intellectual cultivation, although it is of a Bohemian rather than an academic kind. Given a different environment, another training, Mr. Huneker might have emerged as an American Walter Pater."—*London Athenæum* (November 6, 1915).